NUTSHELLS

Equity
and
Trusts

SECOND EDITION

Round Hall's Nutshell, Nutcase, Exam Focus, and Legal Skills Series

NUTSHELL TITLES

Specially written for students of Irish law, each title in the **Nutshell Series** from Round Hall is an accessible review of key principles, concepts and cases. Nutshells are both the ideal introductory text, and the perfect revision aid.

- **Company Law** – 2nd edition by Catherine McConville
- **Contract Law** by Fergus Ryan
- **Constitutional Law** – 2nd edition by Fergus Ryan
- **Criminal Law** – 2nd edition by Cecilia Ní Choileáin
- **Equity and Trusts Law** – 2nd edition by Miriam Dowling
- **Employment Law** by Dorothy Donovan
- **Evidence** by Ross Gorman
- **Family Law** by Louise Crowley
- **Land Law** – 2nd edition by Ruth Cannon
- **Tort** – 2nd edition by Ursula Connolly

NUTCASE TITLES

Round Hall Nutcases are written to give you the key facts and principles of **important cases** in core legal subject areas. Straightforward, no-nonsense language makes Nutcases an easy way to understand and learn key cases.

- **Criminal Law** by Majella Walsh
- **Evidence** by Neil Van Dokkum
- **Tort** – 2nd edition by Val Corbett

EXAM FOCUS TITLES

The series is especially designed to support students in the weeks coming up to exams by providing a unique tutorial approach to answering questions.

- **Criminal Law** by Sarah Carew

LEGAL SKILLS TITLES

The Legal Skills Series helps students master the essential legal and research skills needed to succeed in their studies and in their future careers.

- **How to Think, Write and Cite: Key Skills for Irish Law Students** by Jennifer Schweppe; Ronan Kennedy; Larry Donnelly and Dr Elaine Fahey.

NUTSHELLS

Equity and Trusts

SECOND EDITION

by

MIRIAM DOWLING
BA (Hons)

ROUND HALL  THOMSON REUTERS

Published in 2012 by
Thomson Reuters (Professional) Ireland Limited
(Registered in Ireland, Company No. 80867. Registered Office
and address for service 43 Fitzwilliam Place, Dublin 2)
trading as Round Hall.

Typeset by Carrigboy Typesetting Services

Printed by Ashford Colour Press, Gosport, Hants.

ISBN 978-1-85800-688-8

A catalogue record for this book is available from the British Library.

Acknowledgments

This Nutshell on the law of Equity and Trusts is designed primarily with the student in mind, although practitioners and the general public may also find it useful and informative. It endeavours to explain the key principles and concepts of an often demanding subject in a manner that is easily comprehensible to the reader.

The first edition, which was written by Karl Dowling, has been updated to include a number of significant decisions that have been recently delivered, as well as legislative developments, such as the enactment of the Land and Conveyancing Law Reform Act 2009 and the Charities Act 2009.

The updating of this text would not have been possible without the support and encouragement of Frieda Donohue, Publishing Manager at Round Hall, my colleagues in Pearts Solicitors and my family, Maria, Brian, Ann and Joseph.

I have endeavoured to state the law as of June 1, 2012.

MIRIAM DOWLING

Contents

Table of Cases

England

Northern Ireland

Privy Council

Australia

Canada

New Zealand

United States of America

Table of Legislation

Bunreacht na hÉireann

Irish Statutes

Statutory Instruments

English Statutes

Introduction

HISTORICAL BACKGROUND

In modern times "equity" exerts an influence in every aspect of civil law (e.g. tort, contract and land law) and invokes notions of fairness, justice and good conscience. Williams, in his text *Learning the Law*, 12th edn (London: Sweet & Maxwell, 2002), p.24, makes certain distinctions between equity and the common law, which students may find useful:

> "Equity … is law. Students should not allow themselves to be confused by the lawyer's habit of contrasting 'law' and 'equity', for in the context 'law' is simply an abbreviation for the common law. Equity is law in the sense that it is part of the law of England; it is not law only in the sense that it is not part of the common law."

In terms of historical origin, a system of centralised administration of justice was established in England in 1066. With justice being dispensed in this way, the "common law" quickly developed. The common law had a number of disadvantages and specifically, if an action did not fall within a recognised form of writ, then no remedy was available. By far the most usual remedy was damages, but this is not always an effective remedy, i.e. the plaintiff may seek to prevent the defendant from carrying out an unlawful act.

It is not surprising that there was a growing dissatisfaction with the limited remedies of the common law. From the mid-12th century, the Lord Chancellor began to accept petitions from individual litigants and this resulted in the development of the Court of Equity and Chancery. It facilitated litigants in avoiding the confines of the writ system, thus leading the way for remedies such as specific performance, rescission and the injunction.

However, by the 18th and 19th centuries, common law judges were fiercely resisting the development of equitable jurisdiction on the basis that decisions of the Courts of Equity were inconsistent in nature. Lord Eldon L.C. in the case of *Gee v Pritchard* (1818) 2 Swans 402 at 414 commented that the Courts of Equity were moving swiftly to change their ways:

> "The doctrines of this court ought to be as well settled, and made as uniform almost as those of the common law, laying down fixed

principles, but taking care that they are to be applied according to the circumstances of each case. I cannot agree that the doctrines of this court are to be changed with every succeeding judge. Nothing would inflict on me greater pain, in quitting this place, than the recollecting that I had done anything to justify the reproach that the equity of this court varies like the Chancellor's foot."

In 1858, the Chancery (Amendment) Act (Lord Cairns' Act) came into force and gave chancery judges the power to grant damages in addition to, or in lieu of, the pre-existing equitable remedies. In 1877, the Supreme Court of Judicature (Ireland) Act was passed and this legislation stipulated that both equity and common law were to be applied by judges hearing particular cases.

Conflict between law and equity

Section 28(11) of the Supreme Court of Judicature (Ireland) Act 1877 provides that:

> Generally, in all matters not hereinbefore particularly mentioned in which there is any conflict or variance between the Rules of Equity and the Rules of the Common Law with reference to the same matter, the Rules of Equity shall prevail.

In *Walsh v Lonsdale* (1882) 21 Ch D 9 at 14, Jessell M.R. considered the question of the superiority of equity over the common law in instances of conflict between the two:

> "There are not two estates as there were formally, one estate at common law by reason of the payment of the rent from year to year, and an estate in equity under the agreement. There is only one court, and the equity rules prevail in it."

Fusion of law and equity

Following the enactment of the 1858 Chancery (Amendment) Act (Lord Cairns' Act) and the Judicature (Ireland) Act 1877, it was widely acknowledged that their effect was to fuse the administration of the common law and equity (as opposed to a fusion of the principles of equity and the common law). Indeed, Jessel M.R. in *Salt v Cooper* [1880] 16 Ch D 544 at 549 was of the opinion that:

"But it was not any fusion, or anything of the kind; it was the vesting in one tribunal the administration of Law and Equity in every cause, action, or dispute which should come before the tribunal."

However, the judicial attitude a century later has changed significantly. The view that was put forward by the House of Lords in *United Scientific Holdings Ltd v Burnley Borough Council* [1978] A.C. 904 was that the fusion effected by the Judicature Acts was more than procedural in nature. Lord Diplock was of the opinion that the two systems of common law and equity had merged as a result. This more radical view can be seen in the dicta of Cooke P. in the case of *Attorney General for the United Kingdom v Wellington Newspapers Ltd* [1988] 1 N.Z.L.R.129 at 172:

"As law and equity are now mingled … it does not seem to me to matter whether the duty be classified as equitable or not. The full range of remedies deriving from either common law or equity should be available."

The finding in *United Scientific Holdings Ltd v Burnley Borough Council* [1978] A.C. 904 was subsequently applied by the Irish Supreme Court in *Hynes Ltd v Independent Newspapers Ltd* [1980] I.R. 204, where it was stated by O'Higgins J. at 216 that:

"In Ireland the fusion of common-law and equitable rules was initiated by the Supreme Court of Judicature Act (Ireland), 1877, which contains similar provisions in s.28(7) to those already noted in the English Acts, and was completed by the Courts of Justice Act, 1924, and the Courts (Establishment and Constitution) Act, 1961."

Kenny J. at 221 referred to the House of Lords decision in *United Scientific Holdings Ltd v Burnley Borough Council* [1978] A.C. 904:

"I regard the decision in the Burnley Case as a restoration of a fundamental equitable principle which, unfortunately, has tended to be ignored in many recent decisions."

It should be noted that Hanbury and Martin in *Modern Equity*, 18th edn (London: Sweet & Maxwell, 2009), p.29, rely on both *Lord Napier and Ettrick v Hunter* [1993] 2 W.L.R. 42 and *Tinsley v Milligan* [1994] 1 A.C. 340 in putting forward their proposition that it does not appear that the common law and equity have conclusively fused:

"What can be said is that more than a century of fused jurisdiction has seen the two systems working more closely together; each changing and developing and improving from contact with the other; and each willing to accept new ideas and developments, regardless of their origin. They are coming closer together. But they are not yet fused."

The Maxims of Equity

INTRODUCTION

The maxims of equity evolved from Latin into English and represent the general principles of equity, which are applied by the courts as guidelines as to how to exercise their equitable jurisdiction. These maxims should always be borne in mind on the basis that equitable remedies are discretionary; they often dictate whether or not a remedy will be granted by a court. Mason C.J. in *Corin v Patton* (1990) 169 C.L.R. 540 at 557 described an equitable maxim as being:

> "a summary statement of a broad theme which underlies equitable concepts and principles."

It is important to remember that a number of these equitable maxims may overlap and indeed may contradict one another and therefore must be treated with caution.

HE WHO SEEKS EQUITY MUST DO EQUITY

This maxim looks to the future conduct of the claimant. In order to be entitled to equitable relief, the claimant must act fairly towards the other party and be willing to complete all of his or her own obligations.

In practice, the most common application of this maxim occurs during applications for interlocutory injunctive relief. It is the practice of the courts to require an undertaking as to damages from the applicant prior to the granting of injunctive relief. In *Chappell v Times Newspapers Ltd* [1975] 1 W.L.R. 482, the Court of Appeal refused to grant interlocutory relief in circumstances where the plaintiffs refused to give an undertaking not to behave in a certain manner, with Lord Denning M.R. stating at 502 that:

> "[I]f one party seeks relief, he must be ready and willing to do his part in it."

Similarly, in *Cheese v Thomas* [1994] 1 W.L.R. 129, Nicholls V.C. at 136 stated that:

> "The Plaintiff is seeking the assistance of a court of equity and he who seeks equity must do equity."

HE WHO COMES TO EQUITY MUST COME WITH CLEAN HANDS

This looks to the past conduct of the claimant and requires that the party seeking equitable relief has acted in a bona fide manner. Any evidence of dishonest conduct may invoke the court's discretion to refuse to grant the remedy as sought on the basis of "unclean hands".

It is clear from the decision of the Supreme Court in *Smelter Corporation v O'Driscoll* [1977] I.R. 305 that in circumstances where a plaintiff's conduct towards the defendant is found to be less than honest, a decree of specific performance will be refused. A more flexible approach was taken by the Supreme Court to the application of the maxim in *Curust Financial Services Ltd v Loewe-Lack-Werk Otto Loewe GmbH & Co. KG.* [1994] 1 I.R. 450. As was stressed by Finlay C.J. at 467, the general rule is that the court has discretion to refuse equitable relief on the basis of "unclean hands". However, he held that, "it seems to me that this phrase must of necessity involve an element of turpitude and cannot necessarily be equated with a mere breach of contract".

In order to identify an element of turpitude, Murphy J. in *Kavanagh v Caulfield,* unreported, High Court, June 19, 2002, applied what was described as a public conscience test. It requires the court to make a value judgment by balancing the adverse consequences of granting relief against those that would result if relief were not granted.

It is important to note that the court will decline to intervene on the basis of the "unclean hands" principle unless there is a sufficient connection between the inequitable conduct and the subject matter of the dispute (see *Keating v Keating* [2009] IEHC 405 at 24.)

EQUITY WILL NOT SUFFER A WRONG TO BE WITHOUT A REMEDY

It is important not to interpret this maxim too literally as equitable remedies can only be judicially enforced if the unconscionable behaviour complained of constitutes a legal (as opposed to a mere moral) wrongdoing. Lindley L.J. stressed in *Holmes v Millage* [1893] 1 Q.B. 551 at 555 that:

> "It is an old mistake to suppose that, because there is no effectual remedy at law, there must be one in equity."

In *Edlington Properties Ltd v J.H. Fenner & Co. Ltd* [2006] 1 W.L.R. 1583 at 1595–1596, Neuberger L.J. was of the opinion that the fact that a particular type of right or relief may be equitable "does not … operate as a green light to invent new general or specific rules in order to achieve what one judge might regard as a fair result in a particular case".

Indeed, this maxim is more relevant to the enforcement of trusts, which are equitable in nature.

DELAY DEFEATS EQUITY

This maxim represents the equitable doctrine of laches, which asserts that the law assists the vigilant and not those who sleep. Lord Camden L.C. in *Smith v Clay* (1767) 3 Bro CC 639 at 640 summarised the purpose of this maxim as follows:

> "A court of equity … has always refused its aid to state demands, where a party has slept upon his right and acquiesced for a great length."

It can be said that lapse of time, coupled with circumstances which made it inequitable to enforce the claim, will be sufficient to bar a plaintiff's action (see *McGrath v Stewart* [2008] IEHC 348). In *Fisher v Brook* [2009] 1 W.L.R. 1764 at 1781, Lord Neuberger commented that, "some sort of detrimental reliance is usually an essential ingredient of laches". Furthermore, it has been suggested by McMahon J. in *Victory v Galhoy Inns Ltd* [2010] IEHC 459 at para.34 that the levels of inactivity required to deprive a person of his rights in such circumstances is high and "must be so reprehensible that it approaches dishonesty".

The maxim has been made somewhat obsolete by the introduction of the Statute of Limitations 1957, but it still applies to those equitable claims that are not covered by the statute. It should be noted that delay by itself is never enough and must be accompanied by some prejudice to the defendant.

EQUITY FOLLOWS THE LAW

From this maxim it follows that equity will not permit a remedy that is contrary to the common law or statute. However, certain exceptions apply and in these circumstances equity will take precedence over conflicting rules at common law. Indeed, Cardozo C.J. in *Graf v Hope Building Corporation* (1930) 254 N.Y. 1 at 9 was of the opinion that:

> "Equity follows the law, but not slavishly nor always."

It can be asserted that equity will intervene in an application of the common law if it is believed to be in the interests of fairness to do so. This principle has been illustrated by the case of *McCormack v Grogan* (1869) L.R. 4 H.L. 82, where Lord Westbury indicated at 97 that, "equity will not allow a statute to be used as an instrument of fraud".

EQUITY ACTS IN PERSONAM

This means that equitable remedies are personal in nature, in that they are exercisable against specific persons rather than against particular property owned by them. As Lord Selborne L.C. stated in *Ewing v Orr Ewing (No.1)* (1883) 9 App. Cas. 34 at 40:

> "The courts of Equity in England are, and always have been, courts of conscience, operating in personam and not in rem."

EQUALITY IS EQUITY

This maxim comes into operation where two or more parties claim to have an interest in the same property. In the absence of any agreement to the contrary, equity will assume that they have equal shares. An illustration of this can be seen in the application of equity in the co-ownership of land; in the absence of any evidence of a joint tenancy existing, equity will presume that a tenancy in common exists.

The Supreme Court in *EB v SS* [1998] 2 I.L.R.M. 141 held that this maxim may not necessarily apply in circumstances where an application is brought under s.117 of the Succession Act 1965, with Keane J. commenting at 150 that:

> "[T]he maxim 'equality is equity' can have no application where the testator has, by dividing his estate in that manner, disregarded the special needs ... of one of the children to such an extent that he could be said to have failed in his moral duty to that child."

EQUITY LOOKS ON THAT AS DONE WHICH OUGHT TO HAVE BEEN DONE

This maxim is most commonly applied in the sphere of contract law. Where it is clear that a specific obligation exists, equity then treats that obligation as already having been done, but only in favour of such persons as have an entitlement to enforce the contract and not in favour of mere volunteers.

This is well demonstrated in the case of *Walsh v Lonsdale* [1882] 21 Ch D 9 where a specifically enforceable contract for a lease was treated as being equivalent to a lease and the rights and duties of the parties were regarded as being the same as if the lease had actually been executed.

EQUITY LOOKS TO THE INTENT RATHER THAN THE FORM

This maxim means that equity applies a test of substance. However, it does not mean that legal formalities will not be required by equity. Lord Romilly M.R. in *Parkin v Thorold* (1852) 16 Beav. 59 at 66–67 summarised this principle in the following terms:

> "Courts of equity make a distinction in all cases between that which is a matter of substance and that which is a matter of form; and if it finds that by insisting on the form, the substance will be defeated, it holds it to be inequitable to allow a person to insist on such form, and thereby defeat the substance."

EQUITY IMPUTES AN INTENTION TO FULFIL AN OBLIGATION

Where one party is under an obligation to perform a specified act, but instead does some other act which could be regarded as performance of the obligation, equity regards this as fulfilling the obligation. This maxim forms the basis for the equitable doctrines of satisfaction and performance.

WHERE THE EQUITIES ARE EQUAL, THE FIRST IN TIME PREVAILS; WHERE THE EQUITIES ARE EQUAL, THE LAW PREVAILS

It is important to consider these two maxims together as they are relevant to the question of priority as between competing interests in land. The question of priority of interest in land is principally determined by the doctrine of notice.

These two maxims provide the basis for the doctrine of notice and in its most basic form, it stipulates that a purchaser of land will only be bound by those equitable interests of which he or she had notice—be it actual, constructive or imputed notice (see s.83 of the Land and Conveyancing Law Reform Act 2009, which provides that "[a] covenant, whether express or implied, entered into by a person with that person jointly with another person or other persons shall be construed and is enforceable as if it had been entered into with that other person or persons alone"). Similarly, if both of the parties hold mere equitable interests, then the first in time, i.e. the first to be created, will prevail.

It is important to note that s.21 of the Land and Conveyancing Law Reform Act 2009 has affected the doctrine of notice as it applies to priorities as between competing interests in land. Section 21(1) provides that:

> Subject to *subsection (3)*, a conveyance to a purchaser of a legal estate or legal interest in land by the person or persons specified in *subsection (2)* overreaches any equitable interest in the land so that it ceases to affect that estate or interest, whether or not the purchaser has notice of the equitable interest.

Injunctions

INTRODUCTION

An injunction is an order of the court, granted either at trial or prior to trial, restraining a person to whom it is directed from engaging in a specified act or requiring that person to perform a particular action.

Injunctions are of an equitable nature and were developed primarily to address the deficiency of the common law, particularly the availability of damages exclusively as a remedy.

CLASSIFICATION OF INJUNCTIONS

Injunctions can be divided into core categories; the mandatory injunction, the prohibitory injunction and the quia timet injunction.

1. The **mandatory** injunction involves the court ordering the performance of a particular act.
2. The **prohibitory** injunction restrains the performance or continuance of a specified act.
3. The **quia timet** injunction prevents the apprehended risk of damage from occurring. In order to succeed the applicant must demonstrate a "proven substantial risk of danger" (per Geoghegan J. in *Szabo v ESAT Digifone Ltd* [1998] 2 I.L.R.M. 102).

Injunctions are also categorised in terms of their duration:

1. A **perpetual** injunction is of indefinite duration or will exist until any dispute between the parties has been settled.
2. An **interim** injunction (sometimes also referred to as an **exparte** injunction) is granted pre-trial in the absence of the respondent. As the application is without notice to the other side, the court requires the applicant to act ubberimae fides, i.e. with the utmost good faith.
3. An **interlocutory** injunction is granted prior to the trial of the action or until a further order is made. Its function is to preserve the status quo until the court can hear the dispute.

GENERAL CRITERIA FOR THE GRANT OF INJUNCTIONS

An injunction will only be granted in order to protect a non-trivial interference with a right of the plaintiff. This right may be a legal or equitable right deriving from common law, a right protected by statute or a right deriving from the Constitution or European law.

The granting of injunctions is discretionary, in that even if an applicant demonstrates an entitlement to equitable relief, the court may nevertheless refuse to grant the order as sought. It is proposed to examine the factors which will be considered by the court in deciding whether or not to exercise its discretion for or against the granting of injunctive relief.

It should be noted that the following factors apply to the granting of perpetual, interim and interlocutory injunctions. However, additional considerations attach to interlocutory injunctions and these will be examined in more detail further on in the chapter.

THE ADEQUACY OF DAMAGES AS A REMEDY

The injunction as an equitable remedy was developed by the Court of Chancery in response to the perceived inadequacy or inappropriateness of damages as a remedy at common law. Proof that the party seeking the injunction would not adequately be compensated for the wrong done by an award of damages is now a prerequisite for the availability of injunctive relief.

The seminal Irish authority on the matter is the Supreme Court case of *Curust Financial Services Ltd v Loewe Lack* [1994] 1 I.R. 450 at 469 where Finlay C.J. stressed that:

> "Difficulty, as opposed to complete impossibility, in an assessment of such damages should not, in my view, be a ground for characterising the awarding of damages as an inadequate remedy."

In *Sheridan v Louis Fitzgerald Group Ltd* [2006] IEHC 125, Clarke J. stated that while it would be difficult to calculate damages in that case, any such difficulty fell short of the impossibility identified by Finlay C.J. in *Curust*.

THE CONDUCT OF THE PARTIES

In its discretionary considerations, the court must consider two equitable maxims, namely *"he who comes to equity must come with clean hands"* and *"he who seeks equity must do equity"*.

In *Argyll v Argyll* [1967] Ch. 302 at 332, Ungoed-Thomas J. stated that:

"A person coming to equity for relief … must come with clean hands, but the cleanliness required is to be judged in relation to the relief that is sought."

As a general principle, Finlay C.J. in *Curust Financial Services Ltd v Loewe Lack* [1994] 1 I.R. 450 stressed that if it is concluded that a person has come to court otherwise than with "clean hands", then the court has a discretion to refuse any injunctive relief on that ground alone.

The court also has discretion to refuse equitable relief where one party is seeking to enforce a right against another party, whilst at the same time refusing to fulfil its own obligations to that party.

In *Chappell v Times Newspapers* [1975] 1 W.L.R. 482, the Court of Appeal refused the relief sought on the basis that a contracting party who seeks equitable relief to compel another party to adhere to their contractual obligations must be ready and willing to fulfil its own contractual obligations.

LACHES AND ACQUIESCENCE

Injunctive relief may be refused by the court on the grounds of laches or acquiescence.

In order for laches to apply, two conditions must be satisfied:

1. Unreasonable delay on the part of the plaintiff in the commencement or prosecution of proceedings;
2. In view of the nature and consequence of the delay it must be unjust to grant the relief sought.

Acquiescence requires an assent on the part of the plaintiff in relation to the acts of the defendant. In light of any lengthy delay, it must be unjust in all the circumstances to grant the plaintiff the injunctive relief sought.

In *Archbold v Scully* (1861) 9 H.L.C. 360 at 383, Lord Wensleydale stated:

"… if a party, who could object, lies by and knowingly permits another to incur an expense in doing an act under the belief that it would not be objected to … he may be said to acquiesce."

In *Criminal Assets Bureau v PS*, unreported, High Court, April 12, 2002, Finnegan P. held that where a party has obtained an interim injunction, he is under an obligation to prosecute the proceedings promptly and any delay will entitle the respondent to have the injunction discharged.

Acquiescence has also been linked with the concept of unconscionability (see *Watson v Croft Promo-Sport Ltd* [2008] 3 All E.R. 1171 at 1185).

The general view is that it is not appropriate that specific private rights should be denied in order to protect a generalised advantage to the public at large.

The Supreme Court in *Bellew v Cement Ltd* [1948] I.R. 61 suggested that public convenience should not be a consideration when deciding whether or not to grant injunctive relief to a private individual.

However, in *Alston Transport v Eurostar International Ltd* [2010] EWHC 2747 (Ch.) Vos J. stated that particularly in cases "at the interface of public law and private law", the public interest should be taken into account in determining the balance of convenience where an interlocutory injunction is sought.

JURISDICTION TO AWARD DAMAGES UNDER THE CHANCERY AMENDMENT ACT 1858

The Chancery Amendment Act 1858, or Lord Cairns' Act as it is commonly known, gave the Court of Chancery jurisdiction to award damages for breach of an equitable right.

A "good working rule" for awarding damages in lieu of injunctive relief was formulated by Smith L.J. in *Shelfer v City of London Lighting Co.* [1895] 1 Ch. 287 at 315–316:

"In my opinion, it may be stated as a good working rule that:–
(1) If the injury to the plaintiff's legal right is small,
(2) And is one which is capable of being estimated in money,
(3) And is one which can be adequately compensated by a small money payment,
(4) And the case is one in which it would be oppressive to the defendant to grant the injunction:–
   then damages in substitution for an injunction may be given."

The leading Irish authority in this area is *Patterson v Murphy* [1978] I.L.R.M. 85 at 99–100, where Costello J. laid down the following principles:

"1. When an infringement of the plaintiff's right and a threatened further infringement to a material extent has been established, the plaintiff is prima facie entitled to an injunction. There may be circumstances depriving the plaintiff of this prima facie right but generally speaking, the plaintiff will only be deprived of an injunction in very exceptional circumstances.

2. If the injury to the plaintiff's rights is small, and is one capable of being estimated in money, and is one which can be adequately compensated by a small money payment, and if the case is one in which it would be oppressive to the defendant to grant an injunction, then these are circumstances in which damages in lieu of an injunction may be granted.
3. The conduct of the plaintiff may be such as to disentitle him to an injunction. The conduct of the defendant may be such as to disentitle him from seeking the substitution of damages for an injunction.
4. The mere fact that a wrongdoer is able and willing to pay for the injury he has inflicted is not a ground for substituting damages."

PRINCIPLES GOVERNING THE GRANT OF INTERLOCUTORY INJUNCTIONS

The essential purpose of the interlocutory injunction is to preserve the status quo until the trial of the issues in dispute. Interlocutory orders have their own inherent problems which stem from the fact that the court is being requested to grant an injunction prior to any examination of the legal and factual issues in question. In order to deal with such difficulties, the courts have developed what is referred to as "the balance of convenience test" (see flowchart at the end of the chapter).

The governing principles of this test were first set out in *American Cyanamid Co. v Ethicon Ltd* [1975] A.C. 396 and approved in this jurisdiction in *Campus Oil Ltd v Minister for Industry and Energy (No. 2)* [1983] I.R. 88, where O'Higgins C.J. at 105 summarised the principles as follows:

> "Interlocutory relief is granted to the applicant where what he complains of is continuing and is causing him harm or injury which may be irreparable in the sense that it may not be possible to compensate him fairly and properly by an award of damages. Such relief is given ... for the purpose of keeping matters in *status quo* until the hearing."

It should be noted that the *Campus Oil* test does not have the force of legislation in relation to the framing of the wording, and ultimately, the granting of injunctive relief is discretionary. Edwards J. in *Chieftain Construction Ltd v Ryan* [2008] IEHC 147 at para.7 stated that, "the Campus Oil criteria only represent guidance, albeit guidance that should not be deviated from lightly".

In *Clane Hospital Ltd v Voluntary Health Insurance Board*, unreported, High Court, May 22, 1998, Quirke J. attempted to lay down a comprehensive statement of the principles governing the grant of interlocutory injunctions:

1. Whether or not the applicant has raised a fair, substantial bona fide question for determination.
2. Whether, if the applicant were to succeed at the trial in establishing his right to a permanent injunction, he could be adequately compensated by an award of damages.
3. Whether, if the respondent were to be successful at the trial, he could be adequately compensated by an award of damages for any loss which he would have sustained by reason of the grant of interlocutory relief.
4. If either party or both have, by way of evidence, raised a real and substantial doubt as to the adequacy of the respective remedies in damages available to either party, then where does the "balance of convenience" lie?
5. In some instances there are many "special factors" (usually technical in nature) which may influence the exercise of discretion and the grant of the relief sought.

It is now acknowledged that a departure from the *Campus Oil* test is justified in certain circumstances:

WHERE THERE IS NO ARGUABLE DEFENCE TO THE PLAINTIFF'S CLAIM

There must be clear evidence tendered that this is in fact the case. In *Ryanair Ltd v Aer Rianta Cpt*, unreported, High Court, January 25, 2001, Kelly J. refused to depart from the *Campus Oil* test as the applicant's case had not been shown to be unanswerable.

TRADE DISPUTES

Section 19 of the Industrial Relations Act 1990 stipulates that where certain conditions are complied with, then:

a court shall not grant an injunction restraining the strike or other industrial action where the respondent establishes a fair case that he was acting in contemplation or furtherance of a trade dispute.

Clarke J. in *P. Elliott & Co. Ltd v Building and Allied Trades Union* [2006] IEHC 320 stated that the court must determine if the required conditions necessary for the application of s.19(2) are present at the interlocutory stage with the court doing its best with the evidence available.

DEFAMATION

The courts have shown a reluctance to grant interlocutory relief restraining the publication of possibly defamatory material. The reasoning behind such reluctance is two-fold: first, the granting of such relief is an interference with freedom of expression; and secondly, a defendant has a number of possible defences open to him or her, including privilege, fair comment and justification.

In *Reynolds v Malocco* [1999] 1 I.L.R.M. 289, Kelly J. commented that an interlocutory injunction should only be granted in the clearest of cases, having regard to the importance of free speech. (See also, *Cogley v RTÉ* [2005] 4 I.R. 79.)

RESTRAINING THE PRESENTATION OF A PETITION FOR THE WINDING UP OF A COMPANY

The reasoning behind this exception is that the granting of injunctive relief would infringe upon the respondent's constitutional right of access to the courts.

In *Truck and Machinery Sales Ltd v Marubeni Komatsu Ltd* [1996] 1 I.R. 12 at 27, Keane J. stated:

> "The constitutional right of recourse to the courts should not be inhibited, save in exceptional circumstances, and this applies ... to the presentation of a petition for the winding up of a company."

WHERE THE TRIAL OF THE ACTION IS UNLIKELY

The granting of interlocutory relief will be unavailable where the trial of the action is unlikely as this would be tantamount to concluding the issue.

Lord Diplock in *NWL v Woods* [1979] 1 W.L.R. 1294 at 1307 stated that:

> "Where, however, the grant or refusal of the interlocutory injunction will have the practical effect of putting an end to the action ... [it] is a factor to be brought into the balance by the judge in weighing the risks that injustice may result from deciding the application one way rather than the other."

The principles as set out in *NWL v Woods* have been considered in this jurisdiction by Laffoy J. in two recent decisions and it is clear that Irish courts have accepted that where the grant or refusal of an interlocutory injunction will have

INJUNCTIONS

the practical effect of putting an end to an action, "the balance of the risk of doing an injustice" is a more appropriate test. See *Callanan v Geraghty* [2008] 1 I.R. 399 and *Jacob v Irish Amateur Rowing Union Ltd* [2008] 4 I.R. 731.

MANDATORY INJUNCTIONS

The fact that a mandatory injunction compels a person to perform a specified action, as opposed to a prohibitory injunction which merely compels a person not to perform a specified action, has led to reluctance on the part of the judiciary to grant such relief. This reluctance to grant mandatory injunctive relief is more evident at the interlocutory stage.

There are two types of mandatory injunction:

1. **Restorative**—this is granted to force a party to put right the consequences of his or her actions, i.e. to remove a structure built on another person's property.
2. **Enforcing**—this requires the performance of a positive obligation.

It is correct to say that the principles that apply to the granting of a prohibitory injunction also apply to the granting of a mandatory injunction. However, it should be noted that because the granting of mandatory relief places a positive obligation on one party, a court will require strong and clear evidence of continuing or impending damage before it will grant such an order.

In *Redland Bricks v Morris* [1970] A.C. 652 at 665–666, Lord Upjohn decided that:

> "A mandatory injunction can only be granted where the plaintiff shows a very strong probability upon the facts that grave damage will accrue to him in the future ... It is a jurisdiction to be exercised sparingly and with caution but with the proper case unhesitatingly."

Megarry J. in *Shepherd Homes v Sandham* [1971] Ch. 340 made it clear that a court will be less likely to grant mandatory relief at the interlocutory stage. The court must also be of the opinion that at trial it will transpire that the injunction was rightly granted.

This reasoning was adopted in *Bula v Tara Mines Ltd (No. 2)* [1987] I.R. 95; however, Murphy J. qualified it by commenting that the granting of mandatory relief should not wholly depend on the strength of the plaintiff's case. This is in line with the traditional *Campus Oil* principles.

The Supreme Court in *O'Donoghue v Clare County Council*, unreported, Supreme Court, November 6, 2003, commented that mandatory relief will not be granted at the interlocutory stage if such an order would be tantamount to resolving the case in the plaintiff's favour.

QUIA TIMET INJUNCTIONS

A quia timet injunction operates to prevent an anticipated or apprehended infringement of a plaintiff's rights. This jurisdiction is well established and exists in relation to perpetual and interlocutory, mandatory and prohibitory injunctions. As any actual injury has not yet occurred, the plaintiff will be required to demonstrate a strong probability that the apprehended mischief will in fact arise.

The court in *Attorney General (Boswell) v Rathmines and Pembroke Joint Hospital Board* [1904] 1 I.R. 161 at 171, concluded that:

> "To sustain the injunction, the law requires proof by the plaintiff of a well-grounded apprehension of injury—proof of actual and real danger—a strong probability, almost amounting to a moral certainty that if the Hospital be established, it will be an actual nuisance."

Geoghegan J. in *Szabo v ESAT Digiphone Ltd* [1998] 2 I.L.R.M. 102 gave detailed consideration to the circumstances in which a quia timet injunction will be granted. He made reference to the test formulated in *Attorney General v Manchester Corporation* [1893] 2 Ch. 87 at 110, namely that a plaintiff must demonstrate "a strong case of probability that the apprehended mischief will, in fact, arise". Further, in order for a quia timet injunction to be granted "a proven substantial risk of danger" must exist.

The principles as laid down by Geoghegan J. in *Szabo* now seem to be firmly established and have recently been applied in *Ryanair Ltd v Aer Rianta Cpt*, unreported, High Court, January 25, 2001. Kelly J. confirmed that when deciding whether or not to grant a quia timet injunction, the court must balance the magnitude of the apprehended wrong against the likelihood of its occurrence.

The following are the specific circumstances in which an injunction may be granted:

TO RESTRAIN A BREACH OF CONTRACT

The seminal decision in this area is *Doherty v Allman* (1878) 3 App. Cas. 709, where Lord Cairns indicated that where an injunction is sought to restrain the breach of a contractual term, the relief will be granted as a matter of course.

The reasoning of Lord Cairns in *Doherty* was adopted by the Supreme Court in *Dublin Port and Docks Board v Britannia Dredging Co. Ltd* [1968] I.R.

INJUNCTIONS

136. Ó Dálaigh C.J. stated that where the court was satisfied that the breach of a negative contractual term was imminent, the court should not concern itself with the balance of convenience or the amount of damage.

In the more recent decision in *Premier Dairies Ltd v Doyle* [1996] 1 I.L.R.M. 363, the Supreme Court seemed to depart from the principles as laid down in *Britannia Dredging*, with O'Flaherty J. considering whether or not there was a fair case to be tried and where the balance of convenience lay.

TO RESTRAIN THE COMMISSION OF A TORT

The most common situations in which injunctive relief will be sought is in instances of trespass and nuisance. As trespass is actionable per se and without proof of damage, injunctive relief is a particularly effective remedy.

It should be noted that there is a traditional reluctance on the part of the courts to grant injunctive relief to restrain the publication of allegedly defamatory material as damages are more often than not the appropriate remedy.

TO RESTRAIN A BREACH OF CONSTITUTIONAL RIGHTS

It is a well-established principle that injunctive relief will be granted to restrain the breach of constitutional rights. In *Parsons v Kavanagh* [1990] I.L.R.M. 560, the court granted an injunction on the basis that the activity of the defendant constituted a breach of the plaintiff's constitutional right to earn a livelihood.

CONTRACTS FOR PERSONAL SERVICES

In general, the courts have shown reluctance in granting injunctive relief where an element of ongoing supervision or specific performance of personal services is involved. The courts are far more likely to enforce an undertaking not to work for another employer.

In *Warner Brothers v Nelson* [1937] 1 K.B. 209, Branson J. granted an injunction on the basis that a court will enforce negative covenants where this does not amount to ordering specific performance by requiring the defendant to either work for the plaintiff or not to work at all.

Modern case law has illustrated a tendency to permit the enforcement of contracts for services where an employee is seeking to restrain his dismissal.

Gilligan J. in *Keane v Irish Amateur Swimming Association Ltd*, unreported, High Court, August 6, 2003, ordered that the defendant continue to pay the plaintiff's salary pending the outcome of the proceedings and was restrained from dismissing the plaintiff from her post.

However, in *Davis v Walshe*, unreported, High Court, May 14, 2002, Murphy J. refused an application restraining the defendants from terminating the plaintiff's contract of employment as damages were an adequate remedy.

Dunne v Dun Laoghaire-Rathdown County Council [2003] 2 I.L.R.M. 147 establishes that injunctive relief will be granted to restrain the commission of acts that are detrimental to the public at large.

MAREVA INJUNCTIONS

Mareva injunctions operate in personam preventing a respondent from removing assets from the jurisdiction or dissipating assets in order to defeat judgment against him or her. It does not give the plaintiff proprietary rights over the assets. It is noteworthy that general equitable principles apply and thus the remedy is discretionary.

The jurisdiction for the granting of Mareva injunctions has evolved from the case of *Nippon Yusen Kaisha v Karageorgis* [1975] 1 W.L.R. 1093. The Court of Appeal stated that where there is a prima facie case that the plaintiff is owed money by a defendant within the jurisdiction and he has reason to believe that assets may be dissipated or removed from the jurisdiction, the court may grant an interlocutory injunction preventing the defendant from doing so.

This principle was confirmed in *Mareva Compania Naviera SA v International Bulk Carriers S.A.* [1979] 2 Lloyd's Rep. 509.

In *Third Chandris Shipping Corporation v Unimarine SA* [1979] Q.B. 645 at 668–669 Lord Denning M.R. stated that:

> "[T]hese are the points which those who apply for it should bear in mind:
> (i) The plaintiff should make full and frank disclosure of all matters in his knowledge which are material for the judge to know.
> (ii) The plaintiff should give particulars of his claim against the defendant, stating the grounds of his claim and the amount thereof, and fairly stating the grounds made against it by the defendant.
> (iii) The plaintiff should give some grounds for believing that the defendant has assets here.
> (iv) The plaintiff should give some grounds for believing that there is a risk of assets being removed before the judgment or award is satisfied.
> (v) The plaintiff must, of course, give an undertaking in damages—in case he fails in his claim or the injunction turns out to be unjustified."

As regards the standard of proof required in order to obtain a Mareva injunction, Murphy J. in *Countyglen v Carway* [1995] 1 I.L.R.M. 481 stressed that there must be a "substantial question to be tried". Furthermore, the plaintiff does not have to establish as a probability that his claim will succeed.

Balance of convenience considerations will be different from those which apply to standard interlocutory injunctions. Specifically, it is irrelevant to consider whether or not damages are an adequate remedy. In making its decision the court will give substantial weight to the extent of hardship that the defendant will suffer.

It is necessary for the plaintiff to refer to the intention of the defendant by showing the likelihood of dissipation or removal of assets from the jurisdiction and that it is the defendant's intention to frustrate the enforceability of a debt.

In *O'Mahony v Horgan* [1995] 2 I.R. 411, the Supreme Court held that the plaintiff must demonstrate that it is the defendant's intention to dissipate or dispose of assets for the purpose of avoiding a judgment against him.

As to the question of the defendant's state of mind, O'Sullivan J. in *Bennett Enterprises v Lipton* [1999] 2 I.R. 221 accepted that direct evidence of an intention to evade will rarely be available at the interlocutory stage and so it was legitimate to consider all the circumstances of the case.

Initially, Mareva injunctions were applied to assets held within the jurisdiction of the court where the action was being tried. However, it is now common for courts to make orders which freeze the defendant's assets on a worldwide basis.

Within the jurisdiction a Mareva order will bind any third party who has notice of it. However, worldwide Mareva orders are not binding on third parties outside the jurisdiction as the court does not enjoy jurisdiction over non-citizens.

An extra-territorial Mareva injunction is an order relating to assets outside the jurisdiction of the courts. Kerr L.J. in *Babanaft International Co. SA v Bassatne* [1990] Ch.13 stated that "in appropriate cases, though they may well be rare, there is nothing to preclude our courts from granting Mareva type injunctions against defendants which extend to their assets outside the jurisdiction".

The granting of such an injunction is more likely to be made after judgment has been given in order to remove the risk of the order being made in favour of a party who is wrongly asserting a cause of action. Third parties should not be affected unless enforced by the courts of the jurisdiction in which the defendants are located. See *Babanaft International Co. SA v Bassatne* [1990] Ch.13.

In *Dadourian Group International Inc. v Simms* [2006] W.L.R 2499 the question of when it is appropriate for the courts to grant permission to enforce a worldwide Mareva order in another jurisdiction was examined. The court went on to set out eight guidelines which would be applied when an application to enforce a worldwide Mareva injunction abroad is made. These are known as the Dadourian guidelines.

ANTON PILLAR ORDERS

Whereas Mareva injunctions are intended to prevent the dissipation of assets, Anton Pillar orders are designed to prevent the destruction of material central to the plaintiff's case. The order requires the defendant to allow the plaintiff, accompanied by his solicitor, to enter his premises and to inspect and if necessary take away or copy any material specified.

The purpose of such an order is to secure evidence before its destruction; therefore, the hearing of the application will be on an exparte basis and usually held *in camera*.

In *Columbia Picture Industries v Robinson* [1987] Ch. 38, Scott J. stated that:

> "Anton Pillar Orders are used to prevent a defendant, when warned of impending litigation, from destroying all documentary evidence in his possession, which might, were it available, support the plaintiff's cause of action."

In granting an Anton Pillar order a court must be satisfied that the three conditions as formulated by Ormrod L.J. in *Anton Piller KG v Manufacturing Processes Ltd* [1976] Ch. 55 are present:

1. There must be an extremely strong prima facie case;
2. Damage, potential or actual, must be very serious for the applicant;
3. There must be clear evidence that the defendants have in their possession incriminating documents or items, and that there is a real possibility that they may destroy such material before any application inter partes can be made.

The leading Irish case is *Microsoft Corporation v Brightpoint Ireland Ltd* [2001] 1 I.L.R.M. 481. The plaintiff sought and obtained Anton Pillar orders enabling it to enter the defendant's premises and to inspect, detain and preserve all unauthorised copies of various computer programs. Smyth J. indicated that the orders had been correctly granted as there was strong prima facie evidence of dishonest conduct on the defendant's part, which indicated a likelihood that it would seek to destroy the records.

INJUNCTIONS

BAYER INJUNCTIONS

A Bayer injunction restrains the defendant from leaving the jurisdiction. It is important to note that they are ancillary to Mareva injunctions and Anton Pillar orders. A court will only grant such an order if satisfied that the defendant intends to leave the jurisdiction for the sole purpose of defeating a Mareva or Anton Pillar order already granted against him.

In *Bayer v AG Winter* [1986] 1 W.L.R. 497, the plaintiff obtained Mareva and Anton Pillar orders against the defendant and then sought an injunction as they assumed that he would leave the jurisdiction to evade the orders. Fox L.J. held that the court had jurisdiction to grant such an order if it were just and reasonable to do so. The court stressed that the order should be of limited duration, being no longer than necessary to allow the Mareva and Anton Pillar orders to be served on the defendant.

The leading authority in this jurisdiction is *O'Neill v O'Keeffe* [2002] 2 I.R. 1, where Kearns J. commented that Bayer injunctions should only be granted in the most exceptional circumstances, particularly having regard to the constitutional right to travel. Kearns J. adopted the following criteria:

1. The court must be satisfied that there is a probable cause for believing that the defendant is about to flee the jurisdiction with the intention of frustrating the administration of justice;
2. The jurisdiction should not be exercised for punitive reasons;
3. The order should not be granted where a less restrictive remedy would suffice;
4. The injunction should be of an interim nature and for the shortest possible time period;
5. The proper and effective administration of justice should out-balance the defendant's constitutional right to travel; and
6. The grant of the injunction should not be futile.

Guidelines established in *American Cyanamid v Ethicon* and adopted in *Campus Oil*

IS THERE A SERIOUS QUESTION TO BE TRIED?
That is, the claim must not be frivolous or vexatious and must disclose a recognised cause of action
If so, then consider:
THE BALANCE OF CONVENIENCE

Are damages an adequate remedy for the applicant and can the respondent pay them?

If Yes → Interim injunction will not be granted

If No → Are damages an adequate remedy for the respondent and can the applicant pay them?

If Yes → Injunction <u>may</u> be granted

If No → Maintenance of the status quo —where other factors evenly balanced

Other factors, e.g. social and economic factors

Consider the merits, i.e. relative strengths of the parties' cases

4 Specific Performance

INTRODUCTION

Specific performance is an equitable remedy that compels one party to a contract to fulfil his obligations under that contract. It was primarily developed to deal with situations where damages would not be an adequate remedy. Specific performance, like other equitable remedies, is only granted as a matter of discretion (see *Murphy v Ryan* [2009] IEHC 305 at 10). However, it should be noted that in some instances, notably contracts for the sale of land, specific performance will be granted as a matter of course. In other instances, however, such as contracts for personal services, it is commonplace that the remedy will not be granted. These points are very well summarised by Lord Hoffmann in *Co-Operative Insurance Society Ltd v Argyll Stores (Holdings) Ltd* [1998] A.C. 1 at 9:

> "A decree of specific performance is of course a discretionary remedy ... There are well-established principles which govern the exercise of the discretion but these, like all equitable principles, are flexible and adaptable to achieve the ends of equity, which is, as Lord Selborne L.C. once remarked, to 'do more perfect and complete justice' than would be the result of leaving the parties to their remedies at common law: *Wilson v Northampton and Banbury Junction Railway Co.* (1874) L.R. 9 Ch. App. 279, 284. Much therefore depends upon the facts of the particular case ..."

Specific performance is a personal remedy, in accordance with the maxim *"equity acts in personam"*. Therefore, once a defendant is within the jurisdiction of the court and can be compelled to carry out his obligations, the court may order him to do so even if the subject matter of the contract is outside the jurisdiction. In *Penn v Lord Baltimore* [1750] 1 Ves. Sen. 444, Lord Hardwicke of the Court of Chancery concluded that specific performance could be ordered in circumstances where the subject matter of the contract was outside the jurisdiction of the court.

Since the enactment of Lord Cairns' Act (Chancery Amendment Act (1858) s.2), the courts of equity have the power to make an award of damages in addition to or in lieu of specific performance. See the decisions of Finlay

Geoghegan J. in *Collins v Duffy* [2009] IEHC 209 and *Duffy v Ridley Properties Ltd* [2005] IEHC 314.

CONTRACTS FOR PERSONAL PROPERTY

Stocks, shares and chattels do not usually possess such individuality, rarity or beauty as to convince a court to order specific performance for their transfer. However, the mere fact that the subject matter of a contract is a chattel will not prevent a court from ordering specific performance. In *Phillips v Lamdin* [1949] 2 K.B. 33, the court made an order granting specific performance in circumstances where the defendant had removed a unique antique door from the plaintiff's premises. Croom-Johnson J. was of the opinion that:

> "... this is a case in which the defendant, in the teeth of his contract, has removed something which is not a mere trifle. I entertain no doubt at all that the defendant is liable to replace the door and bring it back. You cannot make a new Adam door."

In *Behnke v Bede Shipping Co.* [1927] 1 K.B. 649, Wright J. made an order for specific performance of a contract for the sale of a ship, being satisfied that the ship was of peculiar and practically unique value to the claimant.

Cohen v Roche [1927] 1 K.B. 169 is authority for the proposition that specific performance will not be granted in circumstances where, according to McCardie J., the subject matter is an "ordinary article ... of commerce and of no special value or interest".

CONTRACTS FOR THE SALE OF LAND

This is the most common situation where the remedy of specific performance is sought and granted as there exists a general presumption that land has a unique and special value which renders an award of damages insufficient. In addition to establishing that a valid contract for the sale of land exists, a claimant must also demonstrate compliance with s.2 of the Statute of Frauds (Ireland) 1695 (the requirement as originally introduced by s.2 of the Statute of Frauds (Ireland) 1695 is now contained in s.51(1) of the Land and Conveyancing Law Reform Act 2009) or that there was some good reason for not insisting on compliance. Therefore, in order for a valid contact for the sale of land to stand, there must exist a note or memorandum in writing of the contract signed by the person to be charged or his lawfully authorised agent.

It was noted by Kingsmill Moore J. in *Godfrey v Power* [1961] 95 I.L.T.R. 135 that:

> "A memorandum must contain all essential terms. The parties, the property, and the consideration must always be ascertainable from it, but it need not contain any terms which the general law would imply."

It was held in *Boyle v Lee* [1992] I.L.R.M. 65 that a note or memorandum of sale must contain recognition of the existence of a concluded contract and not merely use the term "subject to contract".

Furthermore, in *Supermacs Ireland Ltd v Katesan (Naas) Ltd* [2000] 4 I.R. 273, Geoghegan J. noted that whereas only the material terms need be included in the note or memorandum, it is essential that the concluded agreement contain all terms, whether important or unimportant.

Doctrine of part performance

The equitable doctrine of part performance allows a claimant to rely on his own actions to demonstrate the existence of a valid contract. This doctrine will prevent a statute from being utilised as an instrument of fraud in instances where the formalities as required by s.2 of the Statute of Frauds (Ireland) 1695 are not complied with (s.51(2) of the Land and Conveyancing Law Reform Act 2009 provides that s.51(1) does not affect the law relating to part performance or other equitable doctrines). The justification for the doctrine of part performance was set out in *Hope v Lord Cloncurry* [1874] I.R. 8 Eq. 555 at 557 per Lord Chatterton V.C.:

> "The principle upon which the rule in cases of part performance was engrafted onto the Statute of Frauds is, that it would be a fraud on the part of the person who had entered into an agreement by parol for a lease or sale to turn around and say that it did not legally exist."

In *Lowry v Reid* [1927] N.I. 142, the Court of Appeal of Northern Ireland granted a decree of specific performance in circumstances where the plaintiff transferred his property to another on the basis that if he did so, his mother promised to leave his entire estate to him. However, the promised bequest did not materialise. Andrews L.J. pointed out that the acts relied upon must be those of the plaintiff, not the defendant.

The Court of Appeal also held that the acts must be such as must be referable to some contract and it is not necessary that the part performance relied upon be unequivocally referable to the contract in question.

The House of Lords in *Steadman v Steadman* [1976] A.C. 536 ruled that the payment of money may constitute an act of part performance in certain circumstances. However, such payments can usually be repaid and thus no prejudice will exist to justify a grant of specific performance.

In *Howlin v Thomas Power (Dublin) Ltd*, unreported, High Court, McWilliam J., May 5, 1978, McWilliam J., following the decision of the House of Lords in *Steadman,* stated that in certain circumstances, the payment of money could constitute part performance; however, some degree of prejudice to the plaintiff must be demonstrated.

Barron J. in *Mackie v Wilde* [1998] 2 I.R. 578 at 587 was of the opinion that "ultimately the court is seeking to ensure that a defendant is not, in relying upon the Statute, breaking faith with the plaintiff". Further, Barron J. noted that the following elements were essential:

"(1) that there was a concluded oral contract;
(2) that the plaintiff acted in such a way as to show an intention to perform the contract;
(3) that the defendant induced such acts or stood by while they were performed; and
(4) that it would be unconscionable and a breach of the duty of good faith to allow the defendant to rely on the Statute in order to prevent performance of the contract."

The principles set out by Barron J. in *Mackie* were applied by Laffoy J. in *Liberty Asset Management Ltd v Gannon* [2009] IEHC 468. In *Price v Keenaghan Developments Ltd* [2007] IEHC 190 at 7, Clarke J. stated that part performance "was never intended to aid an incomplete oral agreement", and "if the parties are not yet *ad idem* on the essentials of a contract for the sale of land being the price, property, parties and other particulars such as the closing date, then there is no concluded agreement and the doctrine of part performance is irrelevant".

CONTRACTS THAT REQUIRE SUPERVISION

There has been reluctance on the part of the courts to order the specific performance of contracts that require supervision. In *JC Williamson Ltd v Lukey and Mulholland* (1931) 45 C.L.R. 282 at 297–298, Dixon J. stated that "specific performance is inapplicable when the continued supervision of the Court is necessary in order to ensure the fulfilment of the contract".

Recent authorities have suggested that the court will not refuse an application for specific performance merely because it would result in an element of supervision, but it will be one of the factors taken into consideration in determining what relief should be granted.

In *Posner v Scott-Lewis* [1987] Ch. 25, specific performance was ordered to procure the appointment of a resident porter where there had been a breach of a covenant. Mervyn Davis J. held that such an appointment would not require an unusual degree of supervision by the court. Finally, the court recognised that in granting or refusing specific performance, it must have regard to any hardship that may be caused to the parties.

It was not until the case of *Co-Operative Insurance Society Ltd v Argyll Stores (Holdings) Ltd* [1998] A.C. 1 that the House of Lords had an opportunity to address the issue of enforcing contracts that require constant supervision. Here, the plaintiff landlord sought an order of specific performance of a covenant in a lease which required the defendant, an anchor tenant, to trade during normal retail hours. This was in circumstances where the defendant intended to cease trading in the plaintiff's shopping centre. In refusing to grant specific performance, Lord Hoffmann referred to a number of reasons, stating that the "cumulative effect of these various reasons, none of which would necessarily be sufficient on its own, seems to me to show that the settled practice is based upon sound sense":

   (i) such an order would require the constant supervision of the court;
   (ii) there is the possibility that the court would have to make an indefinite series of rulings to ensure the execution of the specific performance;
   (iii) there is a likelihood of imprecision in the terms of the order; and
   (iv) injustice may be caused by allowing the plaintiff to unjustly enrich himself at the defendant's expense.

Lord Hoffman was of the opinion that there existed a distinction between orders that require a defendant to carry on a business and orders which require a defendant to achieve a result; the former being the one that would require the constant supervision of the court.

It is important to note that Costello P. in *Wanze Properties (Ireland) Ltd v Five Star Supermarket*, unreported, High Court, Costello P., October 24, 1997, granted interlocutory relief restraining the defendant from relocating its business from the plaintiff's shopping centre to a new centre. Unfortunately, the matter never went to trial and Costello P. stressed that he was "merely deciding that the plaintiff had made out a strong case that there was a reasonable probability that it would obtain the order it sought". The reasoning adopted by the House of Lords in *Argyll Stores* is convincing in many respects and this view is supported by the dicta of Peart J. and the conclusions that he reached in *Dakota Packaging Ltd v APH Manufacturing BV* [2005] 2 I.R. 54.

Contracts for personal services

Aside from the question of supervision, the courts have shown a reluctance to order specific performance of contracts for personal services in circumstances where the contractual relationship has broken down. The general rule that contracts for personal services will not be specifically enforced is not without exception.

Megarry V.C. in *Giles v Morris* [1972] 1 W.L.R. 307 at 318–319 held that there exists no absolute rule against requiring the specific performance of contracts for personal services, and the tendency of the courts not to grant such relief is more a matter of strong reluctance than absolute prohibition:

> "One day, perhaps, the courts will look again at the so-called rule that contracts for personal services or involving the continuous performance of services will not be specifically enforced. Such a rule is plainly not absolute nor without exception, nor do I think that it can be based on any narrow consideration such as difficulties of constant superintendence by the court."

The principles which need to be considered where a court is effectively being asked to order specific performance of a contract of employment were examined by Laffoy J. in *Ahmed v Health Service Executive* [2007] IEHC 312. Laffoy J. stated that for a variety of reasons the courts have refused to exercise discretion to compel performance of contracts of employment or their terms. (See also, *Carroll v Dublin Bus* [2005] 2 I.R. 184.)

Contracts to build or repair

Leaving aside the reluctance of the courts to order specific performance on the basis that ongoing supervision by the courts would be undesirable, the main difficulty with enforcing contracts to build or repair is that the obligation may be indefinable. One of the most important decisions in this area is that of the Court of Appeal in *Wolverhampton Corporation v Emmons* [1901] 1 K.B. 515 Romer L.J. at 525, held that the court would only order specific performance of a building contract in the following circumstances:

> "... a plaintiff must establish three things. The first is that the building work, of which he seeks to enforce the performance, is defined by the contract; that is to say, that the particulars of the work are so far definitely ascertained that the Court can sufficiently see what is the exact nature of the work of which it is asked to order the performance. The second is that the plaintiff has a substantial interest in having the contract performed, which is of such a nature that he cannot adequately

be compensated for breach of the contract by damages. The third is that the defendant has by the contract obtained possession of land on which the work is contracted to be done."

It was noted by Lord Hoffmann in *Co-Operative Insurance Society Ltd v Argyll Stores (Holdings) Ltd* [1998] A.C. 1 that the courts are more willing to grant specific performance of contracts to build or repair where ongoing supervision by the courts is not necessary.

DEFENCES TO AN APPLICATION FOR A DECREE OF SPECIFIC PERFORMANCE

Whereas some of the following defences go to the contract itself, others are dependent upon the court's discretion as to whether or not to grant a decree of specific performance.

MISTAKE

In general, the presence of mistake will prevent the validity of a contract and in such circumstances specific performance will not be available. Of course, some mistakes are so minor as to not prevent specific performance from being granted. In *Webster v Cecil* (1861) 30 Beav. 62, a grant of specific performance was refused on the basis that the plaintiff/purchaser knew that the defendant/vendor has had mistakenly offered property for sale at £1,250, rather than £2,250 as was intended.

It seems an important consideration whether or not the plaintiff contributed to the mistake (see *Ferguson v Merchant Banking Ltd* [1993] I.L.R.M. 136).

The case of *Tamplin v James* [1880] 15 Ch D 215 at 221 is authority for the proposition that where the mistake is solely on the part of the defendant and the plaintiff has in no way contributed to it, the courts will be reluctant to order specific performance. James L.J. was of the opinion that:

> "[F]or the most part the cases where a Defendant has escaped on the ground of a mistake not contributed to by the Plaintiff, have been cases where a hardship amounting to injustice would have been inflicted upon him by holding him to his bargain."

This reasoning was adopted by Costello J. in *O'Neill v Ryan (No. 3)* [1992] 1 I.R. 166, where he held that there had to be a balance as to the hardship to which the plaintiff and the defendant would be subjected.

Misrepresentation

If the defendant can prove misrepresentation, whether negligent, fraudulent or innocent, this may afford a defence to an application for specific performance. In cases of innocent misrepresentation, the court will examine the surrounding circumstances of the contract, in particular whether or not the contract can be characterised as fair.

In *Smelter Corporation v O'Driscoll* [1977] I.R. 305, the Supreme Court held that the defendant had been placed under a fundamental misrepresentation which had induced her to enter the contract, and in such circumstances, it would be unjust for the court to order specific performance.

Lack of mutuality

The traditional approach of the courts has been that before a contract will be specifically enforceable, it must be enforceable against both parties. In other words, a court will not grant a decree of specific performance against one party if it could not do so at the suit of the other. The classic example is where the suitor is a minor, as in *Flight v Bolland* [1828] 4 Russ. 298, where Leach M.R. commented that:

> "It is a general principle of the courts of equity to impose only where the remedy is mutual."

Price v Strange [1978] Ch. 337 is authority for the proposition that the time for ascertaining whether a want of mutuality exists is the time of the hearing of the claim and not the time that the contract was entered into.

It is important to note that a lack of mutuality does not prevent the court from granting an order of specific performance, but it is a matter to be taken into account when exercising its discretion.

Laches

In general, equity looks unfavourably on those who delay. However, with regard to specific performance, time is not necessarily of the essence, unless the parties have made it so expressly. In *Union Eagle Ltd v Golden Achievement Ltd* [1997] A.C. 515, Lord Hoffmann stated that in cases where there was a failure to comply with an essential condition as to time, equity would not intervene. Usually, the question as to whether or not the delay has caused prejudice to the defendant will be at the forefront of the court's considerations.

Generally, unless the parties have so stipulated, time will not be of the essence to a contract in equity, although the plaintiff may still be entitled to an order of specific performance even after the date for the performance of the contractual obligations has passed. See *O'Connor v McNamara* [2009] IEHC 190.

IMPOSSIBILITY

A court will refuse to grant a decree of specific performance in circumstances where it will be impossible for the defendant to comply with the order. A court of equity will not make an order in vain. Brewster L.C. in *Sheppard v Murphy* [1868] I.R. 2 Eq. 544 at 557 stated that "a Court of Equity cannot compel him to do that which is impossible".

In *Neville & Sons Ltd v Guardian Builders Ltd* [1990] I.L.R.M. 601, Blayney J. approved the decision of the House of Lords in *National Carriers Ltd v Panalpina (Northern) Ltd* [1981] A.C. 675 at 700 per Lord Simon:

> "Frustration of a contract takes place when there supervenes an event ... which so significantly changes the nature ... of the outstanding contractual rights and/or obligations from what the parties could reasonably have contemplated at the time of its execution that it would be unjust to hold them to the literal sense of its stipulations in the new circumstances; in such cases the law declares both parties to be discharged from further performance."

The defence of frustration was considered by Kelly J. in *Ringsend Property Ltd v Donatex Ltd* [2009] IEHC 568, in which it was stated that "the defence of frustration is one of limited application and narrowness" and that "[i]t arises in circumstances where performance of a contract in the manner envisaged by the parties is rendered impossible because of some supervening event not within the contemplation of the parties". Furthermore, in *Aranbel Ltd v Darcy* [2010] IEHC 272, Clarke J. stated at paras 5.2 and 5.3:

> "[W]here a party intends that they are unable to complete a contract for financial reasons and wishes to resist an order for specific performance on the basis of impossibility, then it seems to me to be clear that the onus of proof rests on that party to establish their inability to complete. In addition ... it follows that that party must put before the court all reasonable evidence necessary to allow the court to assess whether there is a true case of impossibility".

Hardship

This can be said to be a purely discretionary consideration of the court. In *Lavan v Walsh* [1964] I.R. 87, Budd J. was of the opinion that a court "will not enforce the specific performance of a contract the result of which would be to impose great hardship on either of the parties to it".

For the circumstances in which hardship or impossibility may provide a defence to a claim for specific performance where the property which the plaintiff contracted to purchase has fallen significantly in value since the date the contract was concluded, consider the decision of Clarke J. in *Aranbel Ltd v Darcy* [2010] IEHC 272.

5 Rectification

THE NATURE OF THE REMEDY

Rectification can be described as a discretionary equitable remedy whereby an instrument that does not accord with the intentions of the parties to it may be corrected (see *Irish Pensions Trust Ltd v CRC* [2005] IEHC 87). Rectification is an exception to the "parol evidence rule" which stipulates that oral evidence is inadmissible to alter a written instrument (it is clear from the decision of Kelly J. in *Irish Pensions Trust Ltd v CRC* [2005] IEHC 87 that rectification is not confined to bilateral agreements). The courts will not rectify the instrument itself, but rather the mistake in the instrument recording the contract. This was emphasised by James V.C. in *Mackenzie v Coulson* [1869] L.R. 8 Eq. 368 at 375:

> "Courts of Equity do not rectify contracts; they may and do rectify instruments purporting to have been made in pursuance of the terms of the contracts."

In a similar vein, Griffin J. commented in *Irish Life Assurance Co. Ltd v Dublin Land Securities Ltd* [1989] I.R. 253 at 260 that:

> "Rectification is concerned with the defects in the recording, not in the making, of an agreement."

GROUNDS FOR RECTIFICATION

Rectification requires a mistake that is common to both parties with the result that the written document does not contain the true agreement concluded between them. The general rule is that written agreements will only be rectified if there has been a common mistake between the parties; unilateral mistakes will not lead to rectification. However, there is an exception that allows for rectification to take place in circumstances where the unilateral mistake is one of fact and not of law—*ignorantio juris non excusat*.

Mutual mistake

Originally, in order to have an instrument rectified, it was necessary to prove that there existed a valid and enforceable contract. In *Mackenzie v Coulson* [1869] L.R. 8 Eq. 368 at 375, James V.C. suggested that:

> "It is always necessary for a plaintiff to show that there was an actual concluded contract antecedent [to the instrument] which is sought to be rectified."

However, the more modern view is that it is not necessary to show that a valid contract exists, but merely that common intention must be demonstrated. In *Monaghan County Council v Vaughan* [1948] I.R. 306, Dixon J. held that rectification is available whenever there is sufficient evidence of common intention with regard to a particular provision of the contract. In reaching his conclusion, Dixon J. relied on the obiter dicta of Clauson J. in *Shipley Urban District Council v Bradford Corporation* [1936] Ch. 375, where the trial judge was of the opinion that the applicant must demonstrate a continuing intention at the time the contract was signed that there was an agreement reached between the parties that would be embodied in a formal document.

In *Rooney & McParland Ltd v Carlin* [1981] N.I. 138 at 146, Lowry L.C.J. held that, in order to rectify a settlement, it must be shown that the parties had a common intention which was not accurately recorded in the written agreement:

> "1. There must be a concluded agreement antecedent to the instrument which is sought to be rectified; but
> 2. The antecedent agreement need not be binding in law ... nor need it be in writing: such incidents merely help to discharge the heavy burden of proof; and
> 3. A complete antecedent concluded contract is not required, so long as there is prior accord on a term of a proposed agreement, outwardly expressed and communicated between the parties ..."

The Supreme Court in *Irish Life Assurance Co. Ltd v Dublin Land Securities Ltd* [1989] I.R. 253 held that in certain cases a lack of precision in relation to alleged common intention will result in the court refusing to grant an order of rectification. Further, in *Ferguson v Merchant Banking Ltd* [1993] I.L.R.M. 136, the court concluded that where the bargain is too imprecise to constitute a contract, the question of rectification of the agreement will be wholly unstatable.

It is important to note that in *LAC Minerals Ltd v Chevron Mineral Corporation* [1995] 1 I.L.R.M. 161, Murphy J. held that rectification cannot be ordered at the suit of a party who was neither privy to the manner in which the agreement was negotiated nor the circumstances in which the error occurred.

UNILATERAL MISTAKE

In circumstances where one party incorrectly records a term of the agreement, but it is bona fide accepted by the other party, the mistake is said to be unilateral and hence no remedy of rectification exists. However, the remedy may be available if it can be shown that the mistake was due to fraud. The limits of the remedy of rectification for unilateral mistake were set out by the Supreme Court in *Irish Life Assurance Co. Ltd v Dublin Land Securities Ltd* [1989] I.R. 253 at 260–261 per Keane J.:

> "... [R]ectification may be granted in cases of unilateral mistake, provided that there has been some element of fraud or sharp practice on the part of the person against whom the relief is sought; or, to put it at its lowest, where it would be inequitable in the circumstances to allow that person to retain a benefit derived from mistake."

In reaching his conclusion, Keane J. adopted the test suggested in *Thomas Bates & Sons v Wyndham (Lingerie) Ltd* [1981] 1 All E.R. 1077, where Buckley L.J. stated that in order to establish a claim for rectification for unilateral mistake, the following elements must be present:

> (i) That one party wrongly believed that the document included or excluded a particular term;
> (ii) That the other party was aware of the mistake;
> (iii) The other party did not draw any attention to the mistake; and
> (iv) That the mistake was calculated to benefit the other party.

Buckley L.J. noted that if the above conditions were satisfied, it would be inequitable to permit the defendant to resist rectification. The four necessary elements set out by Buckley L.J. which a claimant has to establish in order to maintain a claim for rectification on the grounds of unilateral mistake were applied in *Traditional Structures Ltd v HW Construction Ltd* [2010] EWHC 1530 (TCC). See also, *George Wimpey UK Ltd v VI Construction Ltd* [2005] EWCA Civ 77.

A summary of the circumstances in which a court will grant rectification for a unilateral mistake is to be found in the decision of Binnie J. in *Performance Industries Ltd v Sylvan Lake Golf & Tennis Club Ltd* [2002] 1 S.C.R. 678:

"The plaintiff must establish that the terms agreed to orally were not written down properly. The error may be fraudulent, or it may be innocent. What is essential is that at the time of execution of the written document the defendant knew or ought to have known of the error and the plaintiff did not. Moreover, the attempt of the defendant to rely on the erroneous written document must amount to 'fraud or the equivalent of fraud'."

PROOF OF THE MISTAKE

Historically, the standard of proof required for actions in rectification was akin to the standard of proof required in a criminal prosecution (see, for example, *Fowler v Fowler* [1859] 4 De G. & J. 250 at 265 per Lord Chelmsford L.C.); this is no longer the case.

In this jurisdiction, the standard of proof that is required is to the civil standard; that is, "on the balance of probability". Indeed, in *Thomas Bates & Sons v Wyndham (Lingerie) Ltd* [1981] 1 All E.R. 1077, Buckley L.J. was of the opinion that:

> "The standard of proof required in an action for rectification to establish the common intention of the parties is, in my view, the civil standard of balance of probabilities."

Further, he decided that the standard of proof in cases of unilateral mistake should be no different to that in cases of mutual mistake.

The view of Griffin J. in *Irish Life Assurance Co. Ltd v Dublin Land Securities Ltd* [1989] I.R. 253 at 263 seems to accord with the above authority, where he spoke of the plaintiff establishing his case by "convincing evidence":

> "... [B]earing in mind the heavy burden of proof that lies on those seeking rectification, the question to be addressed is whether there was convincing proof, reflected in some outward expression of accord, that the contract in writing did not represent the common continuing intention of the parties on which the court can act, and whether the plaintiff can positively show what that common intention was ..."

In *Boliden Tara Mines Ltd v Cosgrove* [2010] IESC 62, Hardiman J. was of the view that no form of words other than "proof on the balance of probability" should be used.

DISCRETIONARY FACTORS

As with all equitable remedies, rectification is discretionary. Rectification is generally granted where it would be inequitable to bind parties to a bargain that does not reflect their agreement. In the case of *Nolan v Graves* [1946] I.R. 376 at 391, Haugh J. was of the opinion that the jurisdiction of the court to grant rectification "is a delicate jurisdiction which must be exercised with discretion and care". It appears that the factor most likely to influence a court against granting rectification would be in circumstances where a bona fide purchaser for value would be at a loss (see *Smith v Jones* [1954] 1 W.L.R. 1089).

Rescission

6

RESCISSION AS A REMEDY

Rescission is a process by which a subsisting contract, or other disposition of property, can be avoided at the behest of one of the parties to the contract. Rescission has the effect of nullifying the contract "ab initio", which involves the termination of obligation under the contract and the restoration of the parties to their pre-contractual positions.

Even though equitable rescission is distinct from both rescission at common law and contractual rescission, it is useful to look to the law of contract for a clear definition of "rescission". McDermott, *Contract Law* (Dublin: Butterworths, 2001), p.525, puts forward the following definition:

> "Rescission means different things in different contexts. Particularly in the past, it has been used whenever a contract was brought to an end otherwise than by performance. As a matter of contract law, the breach of an important term of a contract allows the party not in default either to affirm the contract, and to sue for damage if appropriate, or on the other hand to elect to treat the contract as repudiated, so that he is discharged from the performance of any further contractual obligations, and may still sue for damages. This has sometimes been described as rescission. It is also possible for a contract itself to provide for circumstances in which parties will be entitled to treat it as discharged."

Equitable rescission is distinguished from contractual rescission and rescission at common law in that it is the court which makes the decision to use rescission as a remedy, rather than the parties to the contract itself. In *Northern Bank Finance Corporation Ltd v Charleton* [1979] I.R. 149, Henchy J. was of the opinion that rescission as a form of relief "will be granted when the court considers that it would be just and equitable to do so in order to restore the parties, at least substantially, to their respective positions".

There exist four grounds for equitable rescission:

- Mistake
- Misrepresentation
- Undue influence
- Unconscionable transactions

It should be noted that mistake by itself will very rarely lead to the rescission of a contract, although mistake induced by fraud or misrepresentation would be a more compelling justification for the granting of an order for rescission. If there exists mistake on the part of one party to a contract, a "unilateral mistake", the general principle of caveat emptor applies.

"Mutual mistake" or "common mistake", on the other hand, arises in circumstances where the parties to a contract reach agreement, but there exists a mistake as to the facts underlying the formation of the contract. Historically, it was believed that there existed a jurisdiction in equity that allowed for the rescission of a contract on the ground of mutual mistake, even though the contract was valid at common law. The principal case supporting this view was the House of Lords decision in *Bell v Lever Bros Ltd* [1932] A.C. 161.

In *Cooper v Phibbs* [1867] L.R. 2 H.L. 149 at 170, Lord Westbury held that:

> "… [i]f parties contract under the mutual mistake and misrepresentation as to their relative and respective rights, the result is, that the agreement is liable to be set aside as having proceeded upon a common mistake."

After *Bell*, the Court of Appeal in *Solle v Butcher* [1950] 1 K.B. 671 at 693 asserted that a wide equitable jurisdiction existed to rescind a contract in circumstances where the mistake did not invalidate the contract at common law. Lord Denning M.R. relied on the decision in *Cooper v Phibbs*, stating that:

> "A contract is also liable in equity to be set aside if the parties were under a common misrepresentation either as to facts or as to their relative and respective rights, provided that the misapprehension was fundamental and that the party seeking to set it aside was not himself at fault."

In this jurisdiction, Costello J. in *O'Neill v Ryan (No. 3)* [1992] 1 I.R. 166 quoted from the judgment of Lord Denning with approval. The decision of O'Sullivan J. in *Intrum Justitia BV v Legal and Trade Financial Services Ltd* [2005] IEHC 190 suggests that rescission on the basis of common mistake at equity is still part of Irish law.

After half a century of the courts struggling to define equity's supposed jurisdiction, the Court of Appeal rejected such jurisdiction in *Great Peace Shipping Ltd v Tsavliris Salvage (International) Ltd* [2003] Q.B. 679. The Court of Appeal was of the opinion that if this area of the law was to be sufficiently clarified, then this could only be achieved by ruling that there exists no jurisdiction to grant rescission of a contract based on common mistake, where the contract was valid at common law.

MISREPRESENTATION

If there exists a degree of fraudulent misrepresentation, the courts have jurisdiction to rescind a contract at common law and in equity. Indeed, the equitable doctrine of misrepresentation was referred to by Lord Philips in *Great Peace Shipping Ltd v Tsavliris Salvage (International) Ltd* as being "uncontentious".

The leading Irish decision on equitable rescission for misrepresentation is the case of *Northern Bank Finance v Charleton* [1979] I.R. 149. Here, a sum of money was borrowed by the defendants from the plaintiff bank and when there was a default on the loan, the bank sued for recovery of the debt, plus interest. The defendants counterclaimed that they had only entered into the loan agreement on foot of fraudulent misrepresentations allegedly made to them by the plaintiff bank. In the High Court, Finlay P. made an order dismissing the plaintiff's claim on the basis that the defendants had been induced into the contract by fraudulent misrepresentations.

When the plaintiff appealed the matter to the Supreme Court, the decision of the High Court was substantially upheld, with Henchy J. stating that:

> "… the purpose of rescission of a contract on grounds of misrepresentation is to restore the status quo ante on the grounds that a voidable contract is to be deemed wholly void ab initio."

It should be noted that where misrepresentation is made innocently, the courts appear to draw a distinction between contracts that have been completed and those that have not. On one hand, if a contract is complete, then rescission will only be granted in circumstances where the misrepresentation was fraudulent. Indeed, in *Brownlie v Campbell* [1880] 5 App. Cas. 925 at 937, Lord Selborne was firmly of the view that:

> "[I]t is not … the principle of equity that relief should afterwards be given against conveyance, unless there be a case of fraud, or a case of misrepresentation amounting to fraud, by which the purchaser may have been deceived."

On the other hand, the view that was taken by the court in *Gahan v Boland*, unreported, High Court, Murphy J., January 21, 1983, was that innocent misrepresentation will ground an action for rescission if it can be established that, "the representation was made by the defendant with the intention of inducing the plaintiff to act thereon and secondly, that the plaintiff did in fact act or rely on the representation". This was the view echoed by the Supreme Court on appeal. In *Intrum Justitia BV v Legal and Trade Financial Services Ltd* [2005] IEHC 190, O'Sullivan J. stated that the representation did not have to be "the main or paramount consideration in the mind of the representee", but it had to be "part of the underlying basis upon which the representee proceeds".

UNDUE INFLUENCE

Equity recognises a number of situations in which intervention by the courts is justified by reason of one party's influence or dominance resulting in a transfer of property for wholly inadequate consideration. For undue influence to arise, there must exist an element of actual dominance of one party over the other. Historically, it has been difficult to define what exactly constitutes undue influence. In *Allcard v Skinner* [1887] 36 Ch D 145 at 182, Lindley L.J. stated that:

> "... the equitable doctrine of undue influence has grown out of and been developed by the necessity of grappling with insidious forms of spiritual tyranny and with the infinite varieties of fraud."

Lowry L.C.J. in *R. (Proctor) v Hutton* [1978] N.I. 139 at 146 was of the opinion that for undue influence to exist "the plaintiff must prove that an unfair advantage has been gained by an unconscientious use of power in the form of some unfair and improper conduct, some coercion from outside, some over reaching, some form of cheating".

Cases of undue influence can be divided into two categories; actual and presumed undue influence. In *O'Flanagan v Ray-Ger Ltd*, unreported, High Court, Costello J., April 28, 1980, the distinction between the two classes was summarised as follows:

> "The cases where a plaintiff seeks to set aside a gift or other transaction on the ground that it was procured by undue influence have been divided into two classes; firstly those in which it can be expressly proved that undue influence was exercised, in which circumstances the Court intervenes on the principle that no one should be allowed to retain any

benefit arising from his own fraud or wrongful act; secondly those in which the relations between the donor and donee have at or shortly before the execution of a gift been such as to raise a presumption that the donor had influence over the donee."

In cases of actual undue influence, Lord Browne-Wilkinson in *Barclays Bank plc v O'Brien* [1994] 1 A.C. 180 at 189 stated that, "it is necessary for the claimant to prove affirmatively that the wrongdoer exerted undue influence on the complainant to enter into the particular transaction which is impugned".

As regards the categories of relationships to which the presumption of undue influence will arise, Jones L.J. in *R. (Proctor) v Hutton*, April 30, 1979 at 7, decided that the presumption applied to "solicitor and client, trustee and *cestui que trust*, doctor and patient or religious advisor and pupil". It is noteworthy that no such presumption arises between spouses. In *Prendergast v Joyce* [2009] IEHC 199, Gilligan J. made it clear that the categories of relationship to which the presumption applies are "neither closed or rigid".

Unconscionable transactions

Equity intervenes to set aside transactions that are made with ignorant persons, in circumstances where an unfair advantage is taken. The doctrine does not apply to gifts (see *Langton v Langton* [1995] 2 F.L.R. 890). The basis of this doctrine was defined by Lord Hatherley in *O'Rorke v Bolingbroke* [1877] 2 App. Cas. 814 and summarised by Gavin Duffy J. in *Grealish v Murphy* [1946] I.R. 35 at 49:

"Equity comes to the rescue whenever the parties to a contract have not met upon equal terms."

Case law has illustrated that before a transaction can be set aside on the basis of unconscionability, a number of preconditions must be satisfied. Peter Millett Q.C. enumerated the necessary preconditions in the case of *Alec Lobb (Garages) Ltd v Total Oil Great Britain Ltd* [1983] 1 W.L.R. 87 at 94–95:

"First, one party has been at a serious disadvantage to the other, whether through poverty, or ignorance, or lack of advice, or otherwise, so that circumstances existed of which unfair advantage could be taken. Second, this weakness of the one party has been exploited by the other in some morally culpable manner … And third, the resulting transaction has been not merely hard or improvident, but overreaching and oppressive."

Some doubt remains about the requirements which must be met in order to have a transaction set aside on the grounds of unconscionability in this jurisdiction remain as a result of the decision of Laffoy J. in *Keating v Keating* [2009] IEHC 405, in which she referred to the fact that the criteria set out in *Alec Lobb (Garages) Ltd* provided helpful guidance in this respect. It is therefore likely that the Irish courts will continue to apply a less restrictive approach to the circumstances in which a claim based on an unconscinable transaction can be established than is the case in England.

Equitable Estoppel

7

PROMISSORY ESTOPPEL

It is important to note that as promissory estoppel is closely related to contract law, and in particular the doctrine of consideration, promises that are not supported by consideration are generally not enforceable. However, there exist exceptions to this.

Promissory estoppel arises to prevent a person from acting upon representations made to another by words or conduct of a fact that causes that party to incur detriment in reliance on the representation. In such circumstances, the person making the representation will be prevented from acting in a manner that is inconsistent with what had been agreed. In the House of Lords decision in *Jordan v Money* [1854] 5 H.L.C. 185 at 210, Lord Cranworth summarised the principle of estoppel in the following manner:

> "... [I]f a person makes any false representation to another, and that other acts upon that false representation, the person who has made it shall not afterwards be allowed to set up that what he said was false."

Further, Lord Cranworth was firmly of the opinion that the doctrine only applied to the representation of existing facts and not representations of future intention. Black J. in *Munster & Leinster Bank Ltd v Croker* [1940] I.R. 185 at 191 adopted the reasoning in *Jordan* and stated that this form of estoppel "only applies to representation of existing facts".

The House of Lords in *Hughes v Metropolitan Railway Company* [1877] 2 App. Cas. 439 moved away from the strict interpretation of promissory estoppel as illustrated in the decision in *Jordan v Money*. Lord Cairns concluded that equity would prevent a person from denying the trust or accuracy of a representation of a future intention when the result would be unconscionable.

Such reasoning was adopted in *Central London Property Trust Ltd v High Trees House Ltd* [1947] 1 K.B. 130, with Denning J. stating that where a promise is made which "is intended to create legal relations and which, to the knowledge of the person making the promise, was going to be acted on by the person to whom it was made and which was in fact so acted on" the court must make certain that the agreement is honoured.

The decision in both *Hughes v Metropolitan Railway Company* and *Central London Property Trust Ltd v High Trees House Ltd* seem to be at variance with *Jordan v Money* in that the House of Lords held that estoppel could only operate where the misrepresentation is of an existing fact.

The principle as developed by the *High Trees* case was subsequently constrained by Denning L.J. in *Combe v Combe* [1951] 2 K.B. 215, where he was of the opinion that it did not "create new causes of action where none existed before".

In recent Irish decisions, the principle of promissory estoppel has been further restricted. In *Association of General Practitioners Ltd v Minister for Health* [1995] 2 I.L.R.M. 481 at 492, O'Hanlon J. stated that "the doctrine of equitable or promissory estoppel cannot create any new cause of action where none existed before". Furthermore, in *Industrial Yarns Ltd v Greene* [1984] I.L.R.M. 15 at 33, Costello J. concluded that in order to establish a claim of estoppel, "the representor must show that what was said or done by the representer influenced both the belief and conduct of the representor to his detriment".

PROPRIETARY ESTOPPEL

Proprietary estoppel arises in order to prevent a person from strictly insisting upon his legal rights where doing so would be inequitable. The doctrine was developed as an exception to the required formalities for the creation of an interest in land, in order to prevent unconscionable behaviour. The principle was summarised by Edward Nugee Q.C. in *Re Basham* [1986] 1 W.L.R. 1498 at 1503:

> "Where one person, A, has acted to his detriment on the faith of a belief, which was known to and encouraged by another person, B, that he either has or is going to be given a right in or over B's property, B cannot insist on his strict legal rights if to do so would be inconsistent with A's belief."

It is not essential that the assurance given was express, but in order to establish reliance, it must be shown that the assurance was "calculated to influence the judgment of the reasonable man" (as per Denning M.R. in *Brikom Investments Ltd v Carr* [1979] Q.B. 467 at 483).

In order to successfully invoke proprietary estoppel: (i) an assurance has to be given; (ii) reliance has to be placed by the other party on that assurance; and (iii) detriment must be suffered as a result.

Whilst the assurance given need not be express it must be made by a party with an intention that it should be relied upon. In *CD v JDF* [2006] 1 I.L.R.M

37, McGuinness J. in the Supreme Court stated that "there must actually be a promise, or at least a reasonably clear direct representation or inducement of some kind", and it was not sufficient merely to allow something to happen.

It can be said that once an assurance on the part of the legal owner has been established, there is a presumption of reliance. In *Wayling v Jones* (1993) 69 P&CR 170 Balcome L.J. was of the opinion that, "[o]nce it has been established that promises were made and that there has been conduct by the Plaintiff of such a nature that inducement may be inferred then the burden of proof shifts to the defendant to establish that he (the Plaintiff) did not rely on the promises". He further stated that it is necessary for there to be a "sufficient link" between the promise relied upon and the conduct which amounts to detriment.

Delany states in *Equity and the Law of Trusts in Ireland*, 5th edn (Dublin: Round Hall, 2011), p.764, that detriment "will be suffered where the assurance on which reliance is placed is withdrawn and it is the fact of detriment having been suffered which will render it unconscionable for the legal owner to insist on enforcing his rights".

It is clear from the decision of Clarke J. in *Bracken v Byrne* [2006] 1 I.L.R.M 91 that the detriment suffered must be substantial in nature in order to be enforced. Furthermore, the requirement that the detriment suffered by a plaintiff must be substantial in nature was also reiterated by O'Sullivan J. in *McDonagh v Denton* [2005] IEHC 127.

There are three instances in which proprietary estoppel can arise:

IMPERFECT GIFTS

Generally, equity will not act to complete an imperfect gift; however, as the case law suggests, the courts will permit the perfection of a gift in favour of a volunteer. In *Dillwyn v Llewelyn* [1862] 4 De G.F. & J. 517, a son had constructed a house on land belonging to his father as he had wished for him to take the property upon his death. In fact the land was left for the benefit of third parties. The House of Lords held that on the basis that the son had incurred substantial expenditure on foot of a promise, equity should intervene to convey the fee simple estate to the son. Kenny J. in *Cullen v Cullen* [1962] I.R. 268 at 282 summarised the position in *Dillwyn v Llewelyn*:

> "The case is an authority for the proposition that a person claiming under a voluntary agreement will not be assisted by a Court of equity but that the subsequent acts of the donor may give the donee a ground of claim which he did not acquire from the original gift."

In *Smyth v Halpin* [1997] 2 I.L.R.M. 38, the plaintiff's father suggested that he build an extension onto the family home as he would inherit the whole property after his mother's death. Subsequently, the property was not left to the plaintiff and he sued claiming a reversionary interest. Geoghegan J. directed that the property be conveyed to the plaintiff on the basis that his father's promise caused him to expend monies in extending the property.

COMMON EXPECTATION

Proprietary estoppel can arise in circumstances where parties have dealt with each other in a certain manner so as to give rise to a common assumption that one party would acquire rights in the other's lands. This principle was elucidated by Lord Kingsdown in *Ramsden v Dyson* [1866] L.R. 1 H.L. 129 at 170 as follows:

> "If a man, under a verbal agreement with a landlord for a certain interest in land, or, what amounts to the same thing, under an expectation, created or encouraged by the landlord, that he shall have certain interests, takes possession of such land, with the consent of the landlord, and upon the faith of such promise or expectation, with the knowledge of the landlord, and without objection by him, lays out money upon the land, a Court of equity will compel the landlord to give effect to such a promise or expectation ..."

In *Plimmer v Mayor of Wellington* [1884] 9 App. Cas. 699, the Privy Council held that a licensee had an interest in property that was compulsorily purchased on the basis of his expenditure on the property.

It is noteworthy that detrimental reliance on a self-induced expectation will not give rise to proprietary estoppel. In *Attorney General of Hong Kong v Humphrey's Estate* [1987] A.C.114, the Privy Council held that in order for estoppel to be granted, not only must the plaintiff have acted to its detriment, but the defendant must have created or encouraged a belief or expectation.

In *Haughan v Rutledge* [1988] I.R. 295 at 303, Blayney J. held that in order for proprietary estoppel to be granted, four requirements must exist: (i) detriment; (ii) encouragement; (iii) expectation or belief; and (iv) no bar to the equity. In refusing the relief sought, he stated that:

> "... [b]ut as that hope and expectation was not created or encouraged by the defendant, the plaintiffs have no claim which can be enforced at law or in equity."

UNILATERAL MISTAKE

A unilateral mistake on the part of one party as regards the extent of his legal right to land can invoke proprietary estoppel. It is important that there exists some degree of detriment to the party who innocently relies on the mistaken assumption. In *Ramsden v Dyson* [1866] L.R. 1 H.L. 129 at 140, Lord Cranworth made the following summary:

> "If a stranger begins to build on my land supposing it to be his own, and if, perceiving his mistake, abstain from setting him right, and leave him to persevere in his error, a Court of equity will not allow me afterwards to assert my title to the land on which he had expended money on the supposition that the land was his own."

Fry J. in the case of *Wilmott v Barber* [1880] 15 Ch D 96 laid down what is known as the five probanda. These provide that a person should not be deprived of his legal rights in land unless he has acted in a manner which would make it fraudulent to insist on them:

(i) The plaintiff must have made a mistake as to his legal rights.
(ii) The plaintiff must have expended some money or done some act on the faith of his mistaken belief.
(iii) The possessor of the legal right must know of the existence of his own right and that it is inconsistent with the right as claimed by the plaintiff.
(iv) The possessor of the legal right must know of the plaintiff's mistaken belief as to his rights.
(v) The possessor of the legal right must have encouraged the plaintiff in his expenditure of monies on the property.

In more recent times, the courts have recognised that the dicta of Fry J. did not constitute a formula which needed to be strictly adhered to. In *Hopgood v Brown* [1955] 1 W.L.R. 213 at 223, Evershed M.R. was firmly of the opinion that these requirements were not intended to be "a comprehensive formulation of the necessary requisites of any case of estoppel by representation".

A useful summary of the current position is contained in the judgment of Patten L.J. in *Lester v Woodgate* [2010] EWCA Civ 199 at para.33:

> "[I]n subsequent cases, the courts have held that it is not necessary for all five probanda to be satisfied in every case or (therefore) for the acts of the party seeking to rely on the estoppel to have been motivated by a mistaken belief as to his rights. Those conditions are a useful test of what might amount to unconscionable behaviour in such a case but they are not intended to apply indiscriminately regardless of the particular facts or circumstances in question."

8 Definitions and Classifications of Trusts

DEFINITION OF A TRUST

Numerous academic commentators and members of the judiciary have attempted to define the term "trust" with varying degrees of success. The most concise definition is suggested by Keeton and Sheridan in *The Law of Trusts*,12th edn (West sussex: Barry Rose Law Publishers, 1993), p.3:

> "A trust is the relationship which arises whenever a person (called the trustee) is compelled in equity to hold property, whether real or personal, and whether by legal or equitable title, for the benefit of some persons (of whom he may be one and who are termed beneficiaries) or for some object permitted by law, in such a way that the real benefit accrues, not to the trustee, but to the beneficiaries or other objects of the trust."

TRUSTS DISTINGUISHED FROM OTHER CONCEPTS OF LAW

It is important that trusts be distinguished from other legal concepts that resemble trusts. The reason for such segregation is threefold: first, to compare the different legal consequences of a trust and the related legal concepts; secondly, to identify the circumstances in which one concept must exist to the exclusion of the other; and thirdly, to identify the circumstances in which a trust may co-exist with any related concept.

BAILMENT

This is a common law relationship that allows for the delivery of goods upon a condition that they be returned when the purpose of the bailment has been carried out, e.g. if you leave your car in to a garage for a service. There are a number of distinctions between a trust and a bailment:

(i) Bailment derives from common law; trusts are creatures of equity.

(ii) Bailment only applies to personal chattels; trusts apply to any type of property.

(iii) A bailor can vary or enforce a bailment; a settlor cannot without a reserved power to do so.

(iv) A bailor cannot dispose of title; a settlor may transfer the title of goods.

AGENCY

There are a number of similarities between the relationship of trustee and beneficiary and principal and agent, in that both trustees and agents have fiduciary obligations and are forbidden from acting for their own benefit. Agency can be distinguished from a trust on a variety of levels:

(i) The trust relationship is proprietary in nature, agency is personal.

(ii) Agency is usually terminated by death, a trust is not.

(iii) There must exist some form of agreement between principal and agent; this is not required between a trustee and beneficiary.

(iv) An agent can expose his principal to liability, unlike a trustee.

(v) A trustee must only carry out the terms of the trust and is not bound to follow a beneficiary's instructions; an agent must adhere to his or her principal's wishes.

(vi) Unlike a trustee, an agent does not have title to goods in their possession.

CONTRACT

Contracts and trusts are fundamentally different concepts. A trust is an equitable proprietary relationship, which can arise independently of agreement; a contract can be described as a personal obligation resulting from agreement between the parties.

(i) Generally a contract cannot be enforced by a third party; however, a beneficiary is always entitled to enforce a trust even though he is not a party to the agreement that created the trust (see *Cadbury Ireland Ltd v Kerry Co-Operative Creamery Ltd* [1982] I.L.R.M. 77).

(ii) A beneficiary under a trust can enforce it in the absence of any consideration given. On the other hand, a contract is only enforceable if supported by consideration.

POWERS

A power is an authority which is vested in a particular person that allows him to deal with or dispose of property that he does not have ownership of. While trusts are of an imperative nature, powers are discretionary. Powers may be legal but trusts are always equitable.

WILLS AND INTESTACY

A personal representative realises and distributes the assets of an estate. The relationship between a personal representative and a beneficiary under a will is similar to the relationship that exists between trustee and beneficiary. Both personal representatives and trustees are subject to fiduciary duties in the performance of their functions.

CLASSIFICATION OF TRUSTS

It is possible to classify trusts in a number of ways, for example by virtue of their objects or how they were created. There is no universal agreement as to the proper classification of trusts; however, the following categorisations reflect the conventional understanding:

EXPRESS TRUSTS

This is created by an express declaration of the testator or settlor either by an instrument inter vivos (during the life of a person) or by will. All express trusts must observe certain formalities and contain a number of essential elements, which are known as "the three certainties".

CONSTRUCTIVE TRUSTS

A constructive trust is a type of trust that is imposed by the court and comes into being irrespective of the subjective intentions of the parties involved. The historical basis for this type of trust was to prevent fraud, but more recently it has been utilised whenever justice and good conscience require it.

RESULTING TRUSTS

The resulting trust, or implied trust as it is sometimes known, arises from the presumed but unexpressed intention of the testator or settlor. Resulting trusts are divided into two categories:

(i) Automatic resulting trusts—where an express trusts fails for some reason, the property will result back to the settlor or estate.

(ii) Presumed intention resulting trust—occurs as a result of an inference drawn by the court having regard to the donor's intentions.

STATUTORY TRUSTS

Statutory trusts are created or implied by statute, with the most common examples being provided for by the Succession Act 1965.

SIMPLE AND SPECIAL TRUSTS

This classification of trusts differentiates between the nature of the duties that are imposed upon the trustees. A simple or bare trust does not impose any duties on the trustees even though property is vested in the trustee. Under a special trust, a trustee is obliged to carry out duties imposed on him by the testator or settlor and therefore takes a more active role in the administration of the trust.

DISCRETIONARY AND FIXED TRUSTS

A discretionary trust empowers the trustee with a degree of discretion in deciding which beneficiaries should be entitled to the trust property. In a fixed trust each of the beneficiaries has a fixed entitlement to a specified share in the trust property.

PROTECTIVE TRUSTS

The essence of this type of trust is to prevent beneficiaries from disposing of any or all of the beneficial interest as long as the trust is in existence.

SECRET TRUSTS

Secret trusts only arise in relation to testamentary dispositions and are intended to enable provision to be made for a specific object or purpose without being revealed on the face of the will. There are two kinds of secret trusts: fully secret trusts and half secret trusts.

CHARITABLE TRUSTS

Charitable trusts are public trusts designed to promote a purpose that is beneficial to society. The purpose of these trusts is to confer benefit on the public at large rather than on a specific individual.

PURPOSE TRUSTS

These trusts are for the benefit of purposes rather than for beneficiaries and as a general rule are invalid. Private purpose trusts are sometimes termed "trusts of imperfect obligation" because the trustees are not strictly obliged to carry out the terms of the trust.

FORMALITIES

While the common law has always erred on the side of formality, equity has generally taken a more informal approach and this applies to the creation of trusts. However, statute has intervened in certain circumstances.

CREATION OF A TRUST INTER VIVOS

No formalities are necessary for the creation of an inter vivos express trust of pure personalty and can be created orally by declaration or transfer. Under s.2 of the Statute of Frauds (Ireland) 1695, the creation of an express trust in respect of land requires a note or memorandum in writing. Some exceptions to this rule apply:

EQUITY WILL NOT PERMIT A STATUTE TO BE USED AS AN INSTRUMENT OF FRAUD

Notwithstanding the Statute of Frauds 1695, the courts will not permit a beneficiary to be deprived of an interest in real estate under a trust in the absence of written evidence, as there is an established principle that equity will not permit a statute to be used as an instrument of fraud. Some evidence of the trust will of course be required. The most frequently cited example of the operation of this doctrine is the decision of the English Court of Appeal in *Rochefoucauld v Boustead* [1897] 1 Ch. 196 at 206 as per Lindley L.J.:

> "[I]t is a fraud on the part of a person to whom land is conveyed as a trustee, and who knows it was so conveyed, to deny the trust and claim the land himself. Consequently, notwithstanding the statute, it is competent for a person claiming land conveyed to another to prove by parol evidence that it was so conveyed upon trust for the claimant, and that the grantee, knowing the facts, is denying the trust and relying upon the form of conveyance and the statute, in order to keep the land to himself."

DISPOSITIONS OF EQUITABLE INTERESTS HELD UNDER TRUST

Section 6 of the Statute of Frauds (Ireland) 1695 provides that the second and all subsequent dispositions of beneficial interests held under a trust must be in writing and not merely be evidenced in writing. It is essential that the document be signed by the person making the deposition.

CREATION OF A TRUST BY WILL

According to s.78 of the Succession Act 1965 a trust created by a will must comply with certain requirements, i.e. that the will be in writing, signed at the foot thereof, with two or more witnesses attesting the testator's signature. Of course, the statutory formalities will not be strictly enforced where the statute is being used as an instrument of fraud.

ESSENTIAL ELEMENTS

Aside from complying with the formalities outlined above, it is not necessary to utilise a precise formula in the creation of a valid express trust. However, certain elements, which have come to be known as "the three certainties" must be present for a valid express trust to exist. These are:

- (i) Certainty of intention;
- (ii) Certainty of subject matter;
- (iii) Certainty of objects.

These "three certainties" were laid down by O'Byrne J. in *Chambers v Fahy* [1931] I.R. 17 at 21:

> "... [i]t has been established that, in order that a trust may be created, the subject matter must be certain, the objects of the trust must be certain and the words relied on as creating the trust must have been used in an imperative sense so as to show that the testator intends to create an obligation."

CERTAINTY OF INTENTION

There exists no formula of words to demonstrate intention to create a trust; not even the word "trust" is required. With regard to certainty of intention, a distinction is drawn between imperative and precatory words. Imperative words place a trust obligation on the donee, precatory words do not. Precatory words are words merely of hope and desire, e.g. "in hope that".

Prior to the case of *Lamb v Eames* [1871] 19 W.L.R. 659, the courts were willing to interpret precatory words as imposing trust obligations; the opposite thinking now exists.

In *Re Humphrey's Estate* [1916] 1 I.R. 21, the testator devised and bequeathed all of his property to his widow, with the remainder to his daughters as his widow should see fit. Ross J. held that the words were precatory in nature and that the widow should take the property absolutely, stating at 24:

"After a devise and bequest in clear and explicit terms, if a trust is intended to be created one would expect that this be done in terms equally clear and explicit."

In *Re Sweeney* [1976–77] I.L.R.M. 88, the testator devised and bequeathed all of his assets to his wife but "subject to the express wish" that she make provision for certain legacies after her death. The court held that the words were merely for her guidance and advice and therefore did not create a valid trust.

CERTAINTY OF SUBJECT MATTER

It is imperative that the property which is the subject matter of the trust and the beneficial interest of each beneficiary in that property be of sufficient certainty. Of course, it is an altogether different matter when the trustees are given discretion in this regard.

In the much-criticised decision of Ungoed-Thomas J. in *Re Golay's Will Trust* [1965] 1 W.L.R. 969, the testator created a trust for his daughter from which she was to obtain "a reasonable income", with Ungoed-Thomas J. stating at 972 that:

"In my view the testator intended by 'reasonable income' the yardstick which the court could and would apply in quantifying the amount so that the direction in the will is not in my view defeated by uncertainty."

In the more recent case of *Hunter v Moss* [1993] 1 W.L.R. 452, the court held that there was no lack of certainty of subject matter where the settler, who owned 95 per cent of shares in a company, formed a trust over five per cent of them, and that the court was empowered to identify the shares in question.

It should be noted that no lack of certainty exists where the maxim "equity is equality" can be applied, e.g. if a testator were to bequeath property "to my two daughters", it is presumed that they will hold the property in equal shares.

CERTAINTY OF OBJECTS

It is important that the objects or beneficiaries of a trust be identified with sufficient clarity so as to enable the trustees and, if necessary, the court, to properly administer the trust, having regard to the settlor's intentions.

In *Inland Revenue Commissioners v Broadway Cottages Trust* [1955] Ch. 20, Jenkins L.J. at 30 was of the opinion that:

"… in order to be valid, a trust must be one which the court can control and execute."

(i) Fixed trusts

In order for a fixed trust to be valid, all beneficiaries must be clearly identified in the trust instrument. This requirement gives rise to the "complete list test", otherwise known as the class ascertainable rule. This test requires the trustees to be in a position to compile a complete list of all the beneficiaries.

(ii) Discretionary trusts

A discretionary trust obliges trustees to distribute trust property to the beneficiaries, but they have discretion in the selection of beneficiaries. Jenkins L.J. in *Inland Revenue Commissioners v Broadway Cottages Trust* [1955] Ch. 20 stated at 35–36 that:

> "... [a] trust for such members of a given class of objects as the trustees shall select is void for uncertainty, unless the whole range of objects eligible for selection is ascertained or capable of ascertainment ..."

It is important to note that the test is whether it can be said with certainty of any potential claimant that he is or is not a member of the class.

In *McPhail v Doulton* [1971] A.C. 424, Lord Wilberforce held that a trust to provide benefits for the staff of Matthew Hall & Co was valid as it was no longer necessary to have a complete list in relation to discretionary trusts.

Budd J. in *Re Parker's Will* [1966] I.R. 309 held that a will, which stated that the income from a trust was to be divided among the testator's "necessitous nieces and nephews" as the executors saw fit was not void for uncertainty, stating that the whole membership of the class must be ascertainable.

In *O'Byrne v Davoren* [1994] 3 I.R. 373, Murphy J. held that the whole class must be capable of being ascertained, but that the court should not permit difficulties in interpretation to render a gift void for uncertainty.

ADMINISTRATIVE UNWORKABILITY

This form of uncertainty was first advanced by Lord Wilberforce in *McPhail v Doulton* [1971] A.C. 424, where he suggested that a trust may fail for uncertainty where the class of beneficiaries is so hopelessly wide as to not form anything like a class.

CONCEPTUAL AND EVIDENTIAL UNCERTAINTY

This denotes that a trust may fail in circumstances where the description used to define a class of beneficiaries is conceptually uncertain. It requires that a mechanism exist whereby it is possible to say with certainty whether any party is or is not a member of a class under the trust.

9 Constitution of Trusts

INTRODUCTION

Completely constituted trusts are those in which the trust property is vested in the trustees for the benefit of the beneficiaries; a trust remains incompletely constituted until the property is vested. A completely constituted trust is binding on the settlor and unless an express power exists to do so, it cannot be revoked. It is important at this stage to note that while a completely constituted trust will be enforced even at the suit of a volunteer, the courts will not enforce an incompletely constituted trust.

A beneficiary can be described as a volunteer if he has not provided valuable consideration as understood at common law or is someone who provides marriage consideration. Natural love and affection is not regarded as valuable consideration and will not suffice to make an incompletely constituted trust enforceable in equity. Whilst a settlement made prior to and in consideration of marriage is regarded as being a valuable consideration, a settlement made in consideration of a past marriage will not. In *Re Greer* [1877] I.R. 11 Eq. 502, a settlement that was made for the benefit of the children of a former marriage was held not to constitute valuable consideration.

EQUITY WILL NOT ASSIST A VOLUNTEER TO PERFECT AN IMPERFECT GIFT

In *Re Wilson* [1933] I.R. 729 at 739 per Johnson J.:

> "A gift is a gift, and, of course, if a donor, while expressing an intention to give something and taking steps in the direction of giving it, has not gone the whole way, the expectant donee has no equity to compel the completion of the gift. This is good sense and good law."

TRANSFER OF TRUST PROPERTY

For a trust to be completely constituted there has to be an effective transfer of property rather than a mere intention to transfer the property. This proposition is well illustrated by O'Donovan J. in *McArdle v O'Donoghue*, unreported,

High Court, June 8, 1999, where the testator had intended to execute a deed of settlement making provision for his children but failed to make any transfer. The court approved *Re Wilson*, holding that the trust was incompletely constituted and that equity could not come to the assistance of volunteer beneficiaries.

Milroy v Lord [1862] 4 De G.F. & J. 264 is authority for the proposition that in order to ensure that a trust is completely constituted, the settlor must have done everything in his power to effect the transfer.

The case of *Re Rose: Rose v Inland Revenue Commissioners* [1952] Ch. 499 qualified the above rule, in that if the settlor has done everything in his power to transfer property to a trust, but not all the formalities were met, without fault of the settlor, the trust will be regarded as completely constituted.

The principle that was laid down in *Re Rose* has been applied subsequently in *Mascall v Mascall* [1984] 50 P. & C.R. 119 and *Brown & Root Technology Ltd v Sun Alliance and London Assurance Co. Ltd* [1996] Ch. 51. In *Mascall*, Lawton L.J. commented that there had been a completely constituted trust as "the plaintiff had done everything in his power to transfer the house to the defendant".

In *Pennington v Waine* [2002] 1 W.L.R. 2075, the Court of Appeal considered the exception to the principle in *Milroy v Lord*, as set out in such cases as *Re Rose*. The donor took the necessary steps, in light of the articles of association of the company, in order to effect a transfer of shares to her nephew. However, due to no fault on the part of the donor, the relevant transfer forms were never delivered as was required. Howarth J. held that as the donor had taken all the necessary steps that were required of her, the gift was valid.

In *T Choithram International SA v Pagarani* [2001] 1 W.L.R. 1 at 11, Lord Browne-Wilkinson stated that:

> "Although equity will not aid a volunteer, it will not strive officiously to defeat a gift."

Re Rose was distinguished by the Court of Appeal in *Zeital v Kaye* [2010] W.T.L.R. 913 in which it held that a purported gift of a share in a company, in which the deceased transferor had a beneficial interest, failed in circumstances in which he had neither completed nor dated a share transfer form. Rimer L.J. stated that the principle in *Re Rose* required that the deceased should have done all within his power to secure the transfer of the share, but in his view he had not done this and the gift failed as an imperfect one.

Declaration of trust by settlor

It is possible for a settlor to declare himself to be a trustee of his own property for the benefit of third parties. However, the court will require an irrevocable declaration of trust to be made, which is a manifestation of the settlor's intentions. Fitzgibbon L.J. summarised the position of the courts in *O'Flaherty v Browne* [1907] 2 I.R. 416 at 434:

> "A voluntary trust may be created by a declaration of trust, or by a complete assignment of the legal ownership of a trustee; but it is impossible to turn an incomplete, conditional, or postponed gift into a trust where there is no intention to create a relationship of trustee and *cestui que trust*."

In *Miller v Harrison* [1871] I.R. 5 Eq 324, the Court of Appeal suggested that in order for a declaration of trust by a settlor to be valid the effect of the declaration of trust must leave no reasonable doubt as to the reason for its execution.

Exception to the rule that equity will not perfect an incompletely constituted trust in favour of a volunteer

The rule in *Strong v Bird*

The rule in *Strong v Bird* [1874] L.R. 18 Eq. 315 stipulates that where an incomplete gift is made during the donor's lifetime and the legal title to the property subsequently becomes vested in the donee, the donor's prior intention is treated as having been perfected, provided that the intention continued up until the donor's death. Most often this rule applies in relation to executors, in whom property becomes vested on the death of the testator.

A mere intention to make a gift in the future or to make a future testamentary gift does not come within the rule in *Strong v Bird*. In *Re Wilson* [1933] I.R. 729, the court noted the importance of such intention relating to specific property. Furthermore, the gift must be perfected in all respects other than the formalities necessary to effect the transfer and the intention must continue up until the time of death.

The application of the rule has also been considered by the New South Wales Supreme Court in *Blackett v Darcy* (2005) 62 N.S.W.L.R. 392, in which Young C.J. rejected the argument that it should not apply because only one of two donees had been appointed an executor.

Donatio mortis causa

A *donatio mortis causa* is the delivery of property to a donee in contemplation of the donor's death. The gift will not be regarded as complete until death occurs. In *Re Beaumont* [1902] 1 Ch. 889 at 892, Buckley J. described it in the following terms:

> "It is an act inter vivos by which the donee is to have absolute title to the subject of the gift not at once, but if the donor dies. If the donor dies the title becomes absolute not under but as against his executor. In order to make the gift valid it must be made so as to take complete effect on the donor's death."

In the case of a chattel, title passes on the death of the donor and it does not form part of the estate. Where the property is realty, the legal title remains vested in the personal representative. The rule that equity will not assist a volunteer arises as the donee can move the court to compel the personal representative to take all the necessary steps to complete his title.

There are a number of requirements that must be complied with before a *donation mortis causa* will be valid.

In contemplation of death

The gift must have been made in contemplation of death and a general appreciation that death is inevitable is not sufficient; however, there need not be an expectation of death. Farwell J. in *Re Craven's Estate (No.1)* [1937] Ch. 423 at 426 was of the opinion that contemplation equates to a situation where "death for some reason [is] believed to be impending".

In *Bentham v Potterton*, unreported, High Court, Barr J., May 28, 1998, it was held that because the plaintiffs failed to establish that the gift was made in contemplation of the donor's death, the court was not prepared to interfere with the disposition of the property under the will.

Delivery of the subject matter of the gift

Maloney C.J. in *Re Mulroy* [1924] 1 I.R. 98 at 100 decided that there must be "a complete parting with the dominion over the subject matter by the donor" and not just mere physical possession. Therefore, handing property to a person for safe-keeping will not suffice.

The gift must have been conditional upon death and revocable

The gift must have been made on the basis that it is revocable and conditional upon the donor's death. Lord Porter M.R. in *Agnew v Belfast Banking Co.* [1896] 2 I.R. 204 at 216 stated that:

"A *donatio mortis causa* is incomplete till death, and depends upon it. If the sick man recovers it is of no avail. No property passes until death."

PROPERTY MUST BE CAPABLE OF FORMING SUBJECT MATTER OF *DONATIO MORTIS CAUSA*

Any property transferable by delivery can be the subject matter for a *donatio mortis causa* and similarly the delivery of documentation, which has the purpose of effecting transfer of property, is sufficient.

In *Sen v Headley* [1991] Ch. 425, the Court of Appeal held that land will pass as a result of the delivery of title deeds. In this case, the delivery of keys to a box containing title deeds was held to be valid delivery of realty.

Resulting Trusts

CHARACTERISTICS OF RESULTING TRUSTS

A resulting trust is a type of implied trust that arises automatically by operation of the law. It is applied in situations in which the transferee is required by equity to hold property on trust for the transferor. In effect, the resulting trust arises to plug a gap in the beneficial ownership of property when the intention of the owner is unclear.

Classically, resulting trusts were divided into two categories as identified by Megarry J. in *Re Vandervell's Trusts (No. 2)* [1974] Ch. 269 at 294:

> "(a) The first class of case is where the transfer of B is not made on any trust. If, of course, it appears from the transfer that B is intended to hold certain trusts, that will be decisive, and the case is not within this category; and similarly if it appears that B is intended to take beneficially. But in other cases there is a rebuttable presumption that B holds on a resulting trust for A ... The presumption thus establishes both that B is to take on trust and also what that trust is. Such resulting trusts may be called 'presumed resulting trusts'
>
> and
>
> (b) the second class of case is where the transfer to B is made on trusts which leave some or all of the beneficial interest undisposed of. Here B automatically holds on resulting trust for A to the extent that the beneficial interest has not been carried to him or others. The resulting trust here does not depend on any intentions or presumptions, but is the automatic consequence of A's failure to dispose of what is vested in him .... Such resulting trusts may be called 'automatic resulting trusts'."

More recently a number of theories have been suggested to challenge the orthodoxy of the distinction made by Megarry J. between the two types of resulting trusts. In *Westdeutsche Landesbank Girozentrale v Islington London Borough Council* [1996] A.C. 669, Lord Browne-Wilkinson was firmly of the opinion that there exists only one type of resulting trust and that it gave effect to the presumed intention of the transferor. Similar views were expressed by Lord Millett in *Twinsectra v Yardley* [2002] 2 A.C. 164. However, *Swadling*

(2008) 124 L.Q.R. 72 has reasserted the view that whilst some resulting trusts arise because of a legal presumption that a trust was declared by a transferor in his own favour, another type of resulting trust arises by operation of law where there is no proof by evidence or presumption of a declaration of trust in favour of a beneficiary.

AUTOMATICALLY RESULTING TRUSTS

An automatically resulting trust is one that arises when property is transferred to another on trust but some of the beneficial interest is not disposed of. It is characterised as a default mechanism that historically was viewed as having nothing to do with the intention of the parties. Such a trust will automatically arise in the following circumstances:

FAILURE OF A TRUST

In the situation where an express trust fails entirely for whatever reason, a resulting trust will arise for the purpose of holding trust property in favour of the settlor or his estate. Express trusts may fail for a variety of reasons and numerous examples are to be found in the case law.

In *Simpson v Simpson* [1992] 1 F.L.R. 601, the transferee of a bank deposit held the deposit on resulting trust for the transferor in circumstances where the latter lacked the requisite mental capacity to make a gift.

In *Re Ames' Settlement* [1946] Ch. 217, property had been settled by the husband's father upon the trusts of marriage settlement, but the marriage was subsequently declared void. Vaisey J. held that after the husband's death, the property was to be held in resulting trust for the executors of the settlor.

One of the most important cases regarding the failure of trusts is *Vandervell v Inland Revenue Commissioners* [1967] 2 A.C. 291 at 313, where Lord Upjohn was of the opinion that:

> "If A intends to give away all his beneficial interest in a piece of property and thinks he has done so but, by some mistake or accident or failure to comply with the requirement of the law, he has failed to do so, either wholly or partially, there will, by operation of law, be a resulting trust for him of the beneficial interest of which he had failed effectually to dispose."

FAILURE TO EXHAUST BENEFICIAL INTEREST

There exists a possibility that circumstances will occur which have the effect of preventing the complete disposal of the beneficial interest under the trust. It is common for property to be transferred to trustees in order to fulfil a specific purpose, i.e. for the education of children. A problem arises in circumstances where the purpose of the trust has been fulfilled, but the trust is not completely exhausted.

In *Re Cochrane* [1955] Ch. 309, Harman J. described a resulting trust as "... the last resort to which the law has recourse when the draftsman has made a blunder or failed to dispose of that which he has set out to dispose of".

In the case of *Re Trusts of the Abbot Fund* [1900] 2 Ch. 326, a trust was created for the provision of two daughters; however, in circumstances where the trust fund was dissipated, a collection was made for their assistance. Sterling J. was of the opinion that the collection fund was never intended to be the absolute property of the sisters and so was held on resulting trust for the subscribers.

This can be contrasted with *Re Andrew's Trust* [1905] 2 Ch. 48, where it was held that once the formal education of the children had ended, the purpose of the trust was complete—no resulting trust arose, rather the dividend should be divided equally among the children. Kekewich J., adopting the thinking of Woods V.C. in *Re Sanderson's Trust* [1857] 3 K. & J. 497 at 503, stated:

> "If a gross sum be given, or if the whole income of the property be given, and a special purpose be assigned for that gift, this Court always regards the gift as absolute, and the purpose merely as the motive of the gift, and therefore holds that the gift must take effect as to the whole sum or the whole income, as the case may be."

SURPLUS OF FUNDS VOLUNTARILY SUBSCRIBED

In *Re Gillingham Bus Disaster Fund* [1958] Ch. 300, a fund was established which provided for the care of the injured following a bus crash. It was held that in circumstances where the Government took responsibility for the welfare of the victims, the surplus monies should be returned to the original subscribers.

In *Re Bucks Constabulary Widow's and Orphan's Fund Friendly Society (No. 2)* [1979] 1 W.L.R. 936, Walton J. decided that voluntary subscriptions to the funds of a society amounted to an outright gift, and as a result, should be distributed amongst those members who still belonged to the society at the date of dissolution. It should be noted that such distribution will only be granted on the basis that there is no other method of distribution prescribed by the terms of the contract between the society and subscriber.

Johnson J. in *Feeney v MacManus* [1937] I.R. 23 held that upon the dissolution of the General Post Office (Dublin) Dining Club, the entire fund must be distributed in equal shares amongst the members of the club or their personal representatives at the time of dissolution.

It now seems clear from the decision of Lewinson J. in *Hanchett-Stamford v Attorney General* [2009] Ch. 173, despite earlier indication to the contrary (see *Re Bucks*), that where an unincorporated association ceases to exist on the death of one of only two members, the last surviving member is entitled to claim the assets of the association which do not vest in the Crown as bona vacantia.

QUISTCLOSE TRUSTS

A useful summary of the circumstances that give rise to a Quistclose trust was given by Lord Millett in *Twinsectra Ltd v Yardley* [2002] 2 A.C. 164 at 184:

> "... [Such] arrangements are commonly described as creating a Quistclose trust ... When the money is advanced, the lender acquires a right, enforceable in equity, to see that it is applied for the stated purpose, or more accurately to prevent its application for any other purpose. This prevents the borrower from obtaining any beneficial interest in the money, at least while the designated purpose is still capable of being carried out."

In *Barclays Bank Ltd v Quistclose Investments Ltd* [1970] A.C. 567 a company, R. Ltd, arranged to borrow monies from a lender "on condition that it is used to pay the forthcoming dividend" that was due. The bank confirmed that the money "will only be used for the purpose of paying the dividend". The House of Lords ruled that in such circumstances, a trust was created of which the bank had notice and upon the failure to pay the dividend, the monies were repayable to the lender.

The principle that was laid down in *Quistclose* was applied by the Court of Appeal in *Re EVTR* [1987] B.C.L.C. 646, with Dillon J. concluding that "on Quistclose principles, a resulting trust in favour of the provider of the money arises where the money is provided for a particular purpose only, and that purpose fails".

Evans-Lombe J. commented in *Copper v PRG Powerhouse Ltd* [2008] E.W.H.C 498 (Ch), whether or not money has been paid subject to a purpose trust is a question of fact. He stated, "[i]f a purpose trust is to be established, it is necessary for the payer to show that the arrangement pursuant to which the payment was made defined the purpose for which it was made in such a way that it was understood by the recipient that it was not at his free disposal".

PRESUMED RESULTING TRUSTS

A presumed resulting trust, or purchase money trust as it is also known, arises where property is transferred to a third party who gives no consideration and an inference arises that the third party holds the property on trust for the grantor.

WHERE A TRUST ARISES FROM A VOLUNTARY CONVEYANCE

Generally, when property is transferred to a person who gives no consideration for it, the presumption arises that the transferee is holding the property on trust for the transferor. However, it is important to note that such presumption can be rebutted by evidence to the contrary.

In *Re Vinogradoff* [1935] W.N. 68, a grandmother made a lifetime transfer of £800 of shares to her granddaughter, with the transferor continuing to receive the dividends. Upon the grandmother's death, Farwell J. in a much-criticised decision held that there existed a presumed resulting trust in favour of the grandmother's estate. This case illustrates that the courts are willing to presume a resulting trust even if this may not be in accord with the transferor's wishes.

In the case of *Standing v Bowring* [1886] 31 Ch D 282 at 287, the plaintiff's widow transferred stock jointly into her name and that of her godson. When she attempted to revoke that transfer, the Court of Appeal concluded that there was ample evidence to show that she had at the time of the transaction intended to benefit her godson:

> "[T]he rule is well settled that where there is a transfer by a person into his own name jointly with that of a person who is not his child, or his adopted child, then there is *prima facie* a resulting trust for the transferor. But that is a presumption capable of being rebutted by showing that at the time the transferor intended a benefit to the transferee."

Section 62(2) of the Land and Conveyancing Law Reform Act 2009 provides that a deed executed after the coming into effect of that part of the legislation will be fully effective without the need for any conveyance to uses. It further states that, "[i]n the case of a voluntary conveyance executed after the commencement of this Chapter, a resulting use for the grantor is not implied merely because the land is not expressed to be conveyed for the use or benefit of the grantee".

JOINT ACCOUNTS

This is a common situation in which one party opens a joint account with a view to benefiting another upon their death. The traditional approach was summarised by Gordon J. in *Doyle v Byrne* [1922] 56 I.L.T.R 125 at 126–127:

> "Where there is a transfer by a person into his own name jointly with that of a person who is not his child or adopted child, of money on deposit receipt there is, *prima facie*, a resulting trust to the transferor."

In *Owens v Greene* [1932] I.R. 225, the deceased had maintained two joint accounts, one for his nephew and one for the plaintiffs, his distant relatives. He retained control over the accounts until his death, making it clear that his wishes were for the monies to go to the plaintiffs upon his death. The Supreme Court held that the plaintiffs, as mere volunteers, failed to rebut the presumption of a resulting trust. The Chief Justice stated that it would not suffice to show a testamentary intention on the part of the deceased, as such a disposition that was testamentary in nature could only be made by will.

More recently, the Supreme Court in *Lynch v Burke* [1995] 2 I.R. 159 overruled the above decision. Here, the deceased opened a deposit account in the joint names of herself and her niece, with the niece signing all of the relevant documentation. O'Flaherty J. was of the opinion that such a joint deposit was not testamentary in nature and therefore was not required to comply with statutory formality. Further, it was held that the niece had a contractual relationship with her aunt and had a legal interest in the monies. O'Flaherty J. also noted that it would be wrong to use the mechanism of a resulting trust to defeat the clear intention of a donor.

REBUTTING THE PRESUMPTION OF A RESULTING TRUST

The presumption of a resulting trust may be rebutted in the following circumstances:

ILLEGALITY OR FRAUD

Symes v Hughes [1870] L.R. 9 Eq. 475, is authority for the proposition that a resulting trust will not arise in circumstances where the trust was created for an illegal purpose. In *Ayerst v Jenkins* [1873] L.R. 16 Eq. 275, Lord Selborne refused to grant the relief sought on the basis that the presumption of a resulting trust could be rebutted by evidence of the plaintiff's own illegality unless the result would be "to effectuate an unlawful object or to defeat a legal prohibition or to protect a fraud".

In the important decision of the House of Lords in *Tinsley v Milligan* [1994] 1 A.C. 340, Lord Browne-Wilkinson stated that illegality can render a proprietary interest unenforceable in certain circumstances, but only where it is necessary for the claimant to rely on the illegality in order to prove that an interest exists.

In *Lowson v Coombes* [1999] Ch. 373, the Court of Appeal held that the claimant was entitled to a beneficial interest in the trust, in circumstances where the trust had been created for an illegal purpose, but it was not necessary to rely on the illegality in order to establish his claim.

INTENTION TO BENEFIT

Where evidence can establish that it was the transferor's intention to benefit the transferee, no resulting trust will arise. This principle is best illustrated by the case of *Standing v Bowring* [1886] 31 Ch D 282, where the Court of Appeal held that where there is ample evidence to demonstrate that the transferor at the time of the transaction intended to benefit the transferee, no resulting trust will arise.

In the recent decision from the British Columbia Court of Appeal in *Romaine Estate v Romaine* [2001] 205 D.L.R (4th) 320 at 335, Levine J.A. stated that "all of the evidence of the donor's intention, written or oral, at the time a transfer that is claimed to be a gift was made, is admissible to determine whether the transfer was a gift".

The principles which apply in relation to rebutting the presumption of a resulting were also set out by Laffoy J. in *Stanley v Kieran* [2007] IEHC 272. The court made it clear that generally the onus of rebutting the presumption of a resulting trust lies on the person asserting that the presumption did not apply, in this case, the defendant.

PRESUMPTION OF ADVANCEMENT

The presumption of advancement arises in circumstances where the type of relationship between the two parties is such that equity imposes an obligation on the donor to make provision for the donee. This principle was well summarised by Viscount Simmons in *Shepard v Cartright* [1955] A.C. 431 at 445:

> "The law is clear that on the one hand where a man purchases shares and they are registered in the name of a stranger there is a resulting trust in favour of the purchaser; on the other hand, if they are registered in the name of a child or one whom the purchaser then stood *in loco parentis*, there is no such resulting trust, but a presumption of advancement. Equally, it is clear that the presumption may be rebutted ..."

The presumption of advancement has been regarded in more recent times as being an outdated concept. In *Stack v Dowden* [2007] 2 A.C. 432 at 467, Lord Neuberger commented that the presumption of advancement "has now become much weakened, although not quite to the point of disappearance".

FATHER AND CHILD

If a father purchases property for his child, there will be a presumption that it was intended as a gift to the child. The case of *Hepworth v Hepworth* [1870] L.R. 11 Eq. 10 at 12 illustrates this principle well, with Malins V.C. stating that:

> "The law is not doubtful that if this had been a transfer to a stranger it would have operated as a trust, but if a gift is made in favour of a child the presumption of law is that it is intended as an advancement or provision for the child."

It should be noted that the presumption also applies in circumstances where a purchaser of property stands in loco parentis to the person in whose name the property is being held.

The majority of the Supreme Court of Canada held in *Pecore v Pecore* (2007) 279 D.L.R. (4th) 513 that the presumption of advancement should only apply to transfers to minor children and not to adult children even if they are dependent on their parents.

HUSBAND AND WIFE

In addition to married couples, this presumption applies to engaged couples who subsequently marry, but not to mere cohabitees. In *RF v MF* [1995] 2 I.L.R.M. 572 at 576, the presumption of advancement between husband and wife was firmly accepted in this jurisdiction. Henchy J. of the Supreme Court was of the opinion that:

> "The equitable doctrine of advancement, as applied to transactions between husband and wife, has the effect that when a husband buys property and had it conveyed to his wife and himself jointly, there is a presumption that the wife's paper title gives her a beneficial estate or interest in the property."

The decision in *RF v MF* makes it clear that a presumption can be readily rebutted by evidence of contrary intention, with Henchy J. stating at 576 that:

> "The presumption of advancement ... is, of course rebuttable. For a rebuttal to be made out, it is for the husband to show, by reference to acts or statements before or around the transaction, that a beneficial interest was not intended to be conveyed in the circumstances relied on."

In *Malone v McQuaid*, unreported, High Court, O'Sullivan J., May 28, 1998, O'Sullivan J. considered that the presumption of advancement will stand unless it has been rebutted on the facts.

It should be noted that as a result of the decision of the House of Lords in *Stack v Dowden* [2007] 2 A.C. 432, where property is transferred into the joint names of a husband and wife, the function of the presumption of advancement is now performed by the presumption of equal beneficial ownership of property held in joint names laid down in that case.

11 Constructive Trusts

INTRODUCTION

A constructive trust arises by the operation of law, and not as a result of either the express or implied intention of the parties to the trust. It is a trust that operates in equity to prevent a person from deriving profit from fraudulent conduct or from taking an unfair benefit from a fiduciary position. Constructive trusts, like resulting trusts, are not required to adhere to the formal requirements of creation as stipulated by the Statute of Frauds (Ireland) 1695.

Edmund Davies L.J. in *Carl Zeiss Stiftung v Herbert Smith & Co. (No. 2)* [1969] 2 Ch. 276 at 300, was of the view that:

> "... [A] constructive trust is a trust which is imposed by equity in order to satisfy the demands of justice and good conscience without reference to any express or presumed intention of the parties."

However, he qualified this definition by stating that:

> "English law provides no clear and all-embracing definition of a constructive trust. Its boundaries have been left perhaps deliberately vague, so as not to restrict the court by technicalities in deciding what the justice of a particular case may demand."

Constructive trusts have often been seen as trusts that arise when fairness demands it. However, it is important to note that it was held by the court in *Lonrho plc v Fayed (No. 2)* [1992] 1 W.L.R. 1 at 9 that the imposition of such trusts "must be based on principle; there must be some relationship between the relief granted and the circumstances which gave rise to it". It is proposed to examine the imposition of constructive trusts in instances: (i) where no fiduciary relationship exists; and (ii) where a fiduciary relationship does exist.

IMPOSITION OF A TRUST WHERE A FIDUCIARY RELATIONSHIP EXISTS

Equity operates to prevent a person who owes a fiduciary duty to another from taking advantage of that situation by making a personal gain. If such circumstances are found to exist and a secret profit has been made, then equity will intervene and any profit will be held on constructive trust for the benefit of the person or persons who should be entitled to such profit.

A constructive trust will arise even in circumstances where the person who made the unsanctioned personal gain acted with the utmost honesty and even if the party to whom the obligations were owed could never have obtained the benefit in question. The rationale for such a strict rule seems to be to prevent fiduciaries from attempting to act in a manner that is inconsistent with their duties. It is noteworthy that the most common fiduciary relationships that arise include: (a) trustee and beneficiary; (b) directors and company; (c) agent and principal; and (d) partners.

Chatterton V.C. in *Gabbett v Lawder* [1883] 11 L.R. Ir. 295 at 299 stated as follows:

> "The fundamental position upon which the doctrine of constructive trust proceeds is, that no person in a fiduciary capacity shall be allowed to retain any advantage gained by him in his character as trustee. His *cestuis que trusts* are entitled to the benefit of any advantage so gained by him, to any addition or accretion to the trust estate which he may have acquired, and to all profit which he may have made by any dealing with it."

PURCHASE OF REVERSION/RENEWAL OF A LEASE

One of the most common circumstances in which a constructive trust will be created is when a trustee of leasehold property purchases a reversionary interest in a lease or obtains the renewal of a lease for himself. This is commonly known as the "doctrine of graft", in that any profit that is made by a trustee is deemed to be "engrafted" onto the trust property.

In *Keech v Sandford* [1726] Sel. Cas. T. King 61 at 63, it was held that in circumstances where a trustee obtained a renewal of a lease in his own name, rather than for the trust of an infant, then the trustee was liable to account to the infant beneficiary for any profits that he received as a result of his lease.

Lord King L.C. was of the opinion that: "This may seem hard, that the trustee is the only person of all mankind who might not have had the lease; but it is very proper that the rule should be strictly pursued."

In *M'Cracken v M'Clelland* [1877] I.R. 11 Eq. 172, Chatterton V.C. held that where an executor was granted a new tenancy in his own name upon the premature surrender of a tenancy belonging to the estate, he held such on constructive trust for the estate.

Chatterton V.C. in *Gabbett v Lawder* [1883] 11 L.R. Ir. 295 at 299 defined the principle as follows:

"It has long been settled by current authorities that a trustee of a lease-hold interest who obtains a renewal of the lease, whether by covenant or custom, or by the voluntary act of the reversioner, comes within this principle, and that he cannot hold the interest he so acquired for his own benefit, but as a constructive trustee of it for his *cestuis que trusts*."

SECRET COMMISSION AND BRIBES

It is a general principle that a fiduciary, when acting on behalf of another, must not accept secret commissions or bribes. Any profit that is made in such circumstances will be susceptible to being held on constructive trust for the party on whose behalf the fiduciary was acting.

The definition of "fiduciary" has been interpreted somewhat liberally over the years. In *Reading v Attorney General* [1951] A.C. 507, a constructive trust was established in favour of the British Army in circumstances where a soldier that had made significant profit from the smuggling of goods was held to be a fiduciary as he had only been able to do this by relying upon the privileges that attached to the wearing of his British Army uniform.

In *Attorney General of Hong Kong v Reid* [1994] 1 A.C. 324 at 332, the Privy Council deemed that when a bribe is accepted by a fiduciary in breach of his duty, such property is subject to a constructive trust in favour of the person to whom the duty is owed. Lord Templeman held that:

"The rule must be that property which a trustee obtains by use of knowledge acquired as trustee becomes trust property. The rule must, *a fortiori*, apply to a bribe accepted by a trustee for a guilty criminal purpose which injures the *cestui que trust*. The trustee is only one example of a fiduciary and the same rule applies to all other fiduciaries who accept bribes."

Lord Templeman went on to say that if the property that represents that bribe increases, the fiduciary is not permitted to take the excess, as no profit is permissible under any circumstances. If, however, the value of the bribe diminishes, the fiduciary will be personally liable for the difference in value.

COMPETITION WITH THE BUSINESS OF THE TRUST

A trustee or any person in a fiduciary relationship must refrain from placing himself in a position where his duty and his personal interest may come into conflict. The most common situation where such a conflict may arise is where a trustee or fiduciary profits from a business that can be said to be in competition with a business carried on by the trust.

Such were the circumstances in *Re Thompson* [1930] 1 A.C. 324, where Clauson J. granted an injunction restraining a trustee from carrying on a business that was in direct competition with the business of the trust of which he was a trustee. It should be noted that this strict approach was due to the specialised nature of the business, that of yacht brokering.

A more lenient approach to this principle was illustrated by *Moore v McGlynn* [1894] 1 I.R. 74 at 89–90. In this case, it was held that even though there did exist some measure of competition between the personal business of the trustee and the business of the trust, no constructive trust would arise. The remedy was simply to order that the trustee should no longer act for the trust. Chatterton V.C. stated that:

> "I am not prepared to hold that a trustee is guilty of a breach of trust in setting up for himself in a similar line of business in the neighbourhood, provided that he does not resort to deception, or solicitation of custom from persons dealing at the old shop."

COMPANY DIRECTORS

Company directors are forbidden from placing themselves in a position where their personal interests are in conflict with the interests of the company or where they derive a secret profit from their fiduciary relationship. This rule was summarised in *Regal (Hastings) Ltd v Gulliver* [1967] 2 A.C. 134 at 144, where Lord Russell of Killowen, applying the principle in *Keech v Sandford*, stated:

> "The rule of equity which insists on those, who by use of a fiduciary position make a profit, being liable to account for that profit, in no way depends on fraud, or absence of bona fides ... The liability arises from the mere fact of a profit having, in the stated circumstances, been made. The profiteer, however honest and well-intentioned, cannot escape the risk of being called upon to account."

In *Industrial Developments Consultants v Cooley* [1972] 1 W.L.R. 443, a constructive trust was imposed by the court in circumstances where the defendant resigned from the plaintiff company for the sole purpose of being awarded a contract in his personal capacity, which he had previously been negotiating, whilst employed by the company, on behalf of the company.

In contrast, the Court of Appeal in *In Plus Group Ltd v Pyke* [2002] 2 B.C.L.C. 201 declined to impose liability on a former director of the company for setting up business with one of the company's customers, in circumstances where he had not used confidential information and had not breached his fiduciary obligations to the company.

It is clear from the judgment of Rimer L.J. in *O'Donnell v Shanahan* [2009] B.C.C. 822 at 839, that liability to account cannot be qualified by reference to whether the impugned transaction was or was not within the scope of the company's business, and he confirmed that the authorities do not support a "scope of business" exception.

AGENTS

The imposition of constructive trusts in response to the activities of agents was set out by Moore L.J. in *Sherrard v Barron* [1923] 2 A.C. 21 at 24:

> "It is equally settled law that it is the duty of the agent to make the fullest disclosure to his principle of all transactions in which the agent is making, directly or indirectly, a profit out of his principle. If this is done and if the principle, expressly or by course of conduct, impliedly assents, the agent can retain the profit."

In *Boardman v Phipps* [1967] 2 A.C. 46, the House of Lords held that even though the defendants were liable for the profits that they had made, they were entitled to recover for the work that they had done.

The Supreme Court of Canada in *Soulos v Korkontzilas* [1997] 146 D.L.R (4th) 214 imposed a constructive trust on the basis that it is essential "to maintain the integrity of institutions dependant on trust-like relationships".

IMPOSITION OF A TRUST WHERE NO FIDUCIARY RELATIONSHIP EXISTS

It is possible for constructive trusts to be imposed in circumstances where no prior fiduciary relationship exists between the beneficiary and the constructive trustee. Furthermore, a third party may be liable in circumstances where he deals in or receives the property of a trust and where he takes it upon himself to act as a trustee and subsequently commits a breach of trust.

VENDOR OF PROPERTY

In circumstances where a vendor enters into a specific contract for the sale of property, the vendor holds that property on constructive trust for the purchaser until completion of the transaction. In *Lysaght v Edwards* [1876] 2 Ch D 499 at 507, Jessel M.R. stated that:

"The moment you have a valid contract for sale the vendor becomes in equity a trustee for the purchaser of the estate sold, and the beneficial ownership passes to the purchaser."

This was the position accepted by Henchy J., in the minority, in *Tempany v Hynes* [1976] I.R. 101 at 114, with the majority being of the opinion that:

"A vendor who signs a contract with a purchaser for the sale of land becomes a trustee in the sense that he is bound to take reasonable care of the property until the sale is completed, but he becomes a trustee of the beneficial interest to the extent only to which the purchase price is paid. He is not a trustee of the beneficial interest merely because he signs a contract."

It is important to note that while the vendor is a constructive trustee of the land, this does not extend to anything substituted for the land, i.e. proceeds from his own insurance policy over the land. In *Rayner v Preston* [1881] 18 Ch D 1, the court declined to order that the vendor and constructive trustee of the land hand over monies that had been paid under his own insurance policy for damage that had been caused to the property as a result of fire. It was held that the risk had passed to the purchaser, and therefore the responsibility fell to him to insure the premises. Pursuant to s.52(2)(a) of the Land and Conveyancing Law Reform Act 2009 a vendor must maintain the property in a reasonable state of repair.

MUTUAL WILLS

Mutual wills commonly arise where two persons make an arrangement to make similar wills disposing of their assets in a particular way. It is essential that they intend that the wills be irrevocably binding on them. A constructive trust will arise in circumstances where the surviving party subsequently alters their will, thus giving effect to the arrangement provided for in the mutual wills.

In *Re Oldham* [1925] Ch. 75, the court decided that the mere fact that two wills are made at the same time does not automatically give rise to them being deemed mutual wills. There must be an agreement between the parties that the wills are irrevocable by the survivor.

A liberal approach was taken by Nourse J. in *Re Cleaver* [1981] 1 W.L.R. 939, where it was held that the making of similar wills at the same time, and the later simultaneous alteration of the wills, led to a presumption that mutual wills had been made. The Court of Appeal in *Re Goodchild* [1996] 1 W.L.R. 1216 (CA) at 1225, per Leggatt J. deciding that:

"A key feature of the concept of mutual wills is the irrevocability of the mutual intentions. Not only must they be binding when made, but the testators must have undertaken, and so must be bound, not to change their intentions after the death of the first testator."

INTERMEDDLING IN A TRUST

If an individual takes it upon himself to assume the obligations of a trustee and in essence meddles in the business of the trust or engages in activities that are reserved for trustees, he may be deemed to be a "trustee de son tort"—a trustee of his own wrong. The principle was described by Smith L.J. in *Mara v Browne* [1896] 1 Ch. 199 at 209 as follows:

"Now, what constitutes a trustee de son tort? It appears to me if one, not being a trustee and not having the authority from a trustee, takes upon himself to intermeddle with trust matters or to do acts characteristic of the office of trustee, he may therefore make himself what is called in law a trustee of his own wrong—i.e. a trustee de son tort, or, as it is also termed, a constructive trustee."

An individual who has been held by the courts to have established himself in such a role is then exposed to all of the liabilities that a bona fide trustee would be exposed to and owes the trust a fiduciary duty.

KNOWING ASSISTANCE

Dishonest assistance in a breach of trust will expose those persons responsible to liability as constructive trustees. The imposition of liability in such circumstances was set out by Lord Nicholls in *Royal Brunei Airlines Snd Bhd v Tan Kok Ming* [1995] 2 A.C. 378 at 392 as follows:

"A liability in equity to make good resulting loss attaches to a person who dishonestly procures or assists in a breach of trust of fiduciary obligation ... In this regard dishonesty on the part of the third party would seem to be a sufficient basis for his liability, irrespective of the state of mind of the trustee who was in breach of the trust."

In his judgment, Peter Gibson J. in *Baden Delvaux and Lecuit v Société Générale pour Favoriser le Developpement du Commerce et de l'Industrie en France SA* [1993] 1 W.L.R. 509 set out a classification of knowledge:

(i) Actual knowledge;
(ii) Wilfully shutting one's eyes to the obvious;

(iii) Wilfully and recklessly failing to make such inquiries as an honest and reasonable man would make;

(iv) Knowledge of circumstances which would indicate the facts to an honest and reasonable man; and

(v) Knowledge of circumstances which would put an honest and reasonable man on inquiry.

Lord Nicholls in *Royal Brunei Airlines Snd Bhd v Tan Kok Ming* [1995] 2 A.C. 378 at 389 was of the opinion that it is not enough that the defendant is aware that the transfer of property is in breach of trust; it is essential that the defendant acts dishonestly:

> "The standard of what constitutes honest conduct is not subjective ... If a person knowingly appropriates another's property, he will not escape a finding of dishonesty simply because he sees nothing wrong in such behaviour."

There has been much debate as to whether this approach is a thoroughly objective concept, which does not require any subjective knowledge. Indeed, in *Twinsectra Ltd v Yardley* [2002] 2 A.C. 164, the House of Lords disagreed as to whether or not Lord Nicholls had intended to lay down a purely objective test in relation to dishonesty.

Academic commentary in the wake of the *Twinsectra* case favoured the dissent of Lord Millet. Some measure of clarity has been restored by the decision of the Privy Council in *Barlow Clowes International Ltd (in liquidation) v Eurotrust International Limited* [2006] 1 W.L.R. 1476, wherein Lord Hoffman held that the state of mind arising on the facts of this case was one which by ordinary standards would be considered dishonest, stating that:

> "The reference to 'what he knows would offend normally accepted standards of honest conduct' meant only that his knowledge of the transaction had to be such as to render his participation contrary to normal acceptable standards of honest conduct. It did not require that he should have had reflections about what those normally acceptable standards were."

It remains to be seen whether or not the objective approach as favoured by Lord Nicholls will be adopted by the courts in this jurisdiction.

KNOWING RECEIPT

The receipt of misapplied trust property may give rise to a constructive trust, in that the person receiving such property, and satisfying the relevant knowledge requirement, can be held liable as a constructive trustee. A similar result will occur in circumstances where a recipient deals with trust property in a manner that he knows is inconsistent with the provisions of the trust. Millet J. in *Agip (Africa) Ltd v Jackson* [1990] Ch. 265 at 291 distinguished two situations in which knowing receipt of trust property may occur:

> "The first is concerned with the person who receives for his own benefit trust property transferred to him in breach of trust. He is liable as a constructive trustee if he received it with notice, actual or constructive ... The second and in my judgment, distinct class of case is that of the person, usually an agent of the trustees, who receives the trust property lawfully and not for his own benefit but who then either misappropriates it or otherwise deals with it in a manner which is inconsistent with the trust. He is liable to account as a constructive trustee if he received the property knowing it to be such."

As with dishonest assistance in a breach of trust, the degree of knowledge required to prove knowing receipt has led to much judicial discussion. In *Belmont Finance Corporation v Williams Furniture Ltd (No. 2)* [1980] 1 All E.R. 393 CA, Buckley L.J. held that actual or constructive knowledge of the breach of trust would suffice.

However, subsequently in *Re Montagu's Settlement Trusts* [1987] Ch. 264, Megarry V.C. favoured the imposition of a constructive trust only where the recipient possessed actual knowledge of the breach of trust.

More recently, in *Re Frederick Inns* [1994] I.L.R.M. 387, the Supreme Court held that the Revenue Commissioners held tax payments on constructive trust in circumstances where they had received such monies from an insolvent company and as the status of the company was a matter of public record, they had constructive notice of the insolvency.

A similar view was taken by the court in *Ulster Factors Ltd v Entoglen Ltd*, unreported, High Court, Laffoy J., February 21, 1997. Laffoy J., in considering the question as to the degree of knowledge necessary to establish liability for knowing receipt, stated that:

> "[W]hat renders the recipient of or the dealer of funds which are being misapplied in breach of the fiduciary duties of the directors of a company as constructive trustee is knowledge, actual or constructive, of the breach of trust."

It should be noted that in the recent case of *Bank of Credit and Commerce International (Overseas) Ltd v Akindele* [2001] Ch. 437, the Court of Appeal advanced the proposition that dishonesty is not a prerequisite to the imposition of liability for knowing receipt.

The alternative approaches to the imposition of liability in cases of knowing receipt were considered in some detail by Laffoy J. in *Fyffes plc v DCC plc* [2005] IEHC 477. The court expressed the view that in putting forward the unconscionability test in *Akindele*, Nourse L.J. was adopting a stricter, not a laxer, test than constructive notice. Laffoy J. concluded that in the circumstances it was not necessary for her to decide between the application of the *Akindele* unconscionability test or the *Belomot/Frederick Inns* actual or constructive knowledge test, although earlier in her judgment she did refer to *Frederick Inns* as "a decision by which the court is bound".

NEW MODEL CONSTRUCTIVE TRUST

The new model constructive trust was instituted by Lord Denning in the House of Lords decision in *Hussey v Palmer* [1972] 1 W.L.R. 1286 at 1290, where he stated that equity would impose a constructive trust "whenever justice and good conscience requires it".

In this jurisdiction, Barron J. in *NAD v TD* [1985] I.L.R.M. 153 at 160 seemed to adopt the reasoning of Lord Denning:

> "The constructive trust is imposed by operation of law independently of intention in order to satisfy the demands of justice and good conscience. Its imposition is dependent upon the conduct of the person upon whom the trust is imposed and prevents him from acting in breach of good faith. There is no fixed set of circumstances in which such a trust is imposed."

In *HKN Invest Oy v Incotrade Pvt Ltd* [1993] 3 I.R. 152, Costello J. held that "where a person ... holds property in circumstances which in equity and good conscience should be held to be enjoyed by another he will be compelled to hold the property in trust for another".

Budd J. in *Dublin Corporation v Ancient Guild of Incorporated Brick and Stone Layers and Allied Trades Union*, unreported, High Court, Budd J., March 6, 1996, seemed to adopt a more cautious approach to what he termed "the nebulous touchstone" of justice and good conscience. He was of the opinion that the imposition of constructive trusts "does not leave it open to the court to indulge random notions of what is fair and just as a matter of abstract morality".

In the most recent decision, Barr J. in *Kelly v Cahill* [2001] 2 I.L.R.M. 205 at 62 expressed the view that "a 'new model' constructive trust ... the purpose of which is to prevent unjust enrichment is an equitable concept which deserves recognition in Irish law".

12

Secret Trusts

INTRODUCTION

Secret trusts arise only in relation to testamentary dispositions and can be divided into two categories: the fully secret trust and the half secret trust. The purpose of a secret trust is to keep the identity of the object or beneficiaries under the trust a secret. Lord Wood V.C. in *McCormack v Grogan* [1869] L.R. 4 H.L. 82 defined a secret trust as:

> "Where a person either expressly promises, or by his silence implies, that he will carry out the testator's intentions into effect, and the property is left upon the faith of that promise or undertaking, it is in effect a case of trust."

Secret trusts were characterised as constructive in nature by Patten L.J. in *De Bruyne v De Bruyne* [2010] 2 F.L.R. 1240, where he commented that in such cases, although the intended beneficiary does not rely in any sense on an agreement, equity will regard it as against conscience for the owner of the property to deny the terms on which he received it.

Secret trusts allow the testator the opportunity to avoid the necessity of specifying, at the time the will is created, precisely how the trust is to be administered. The usual method of executing such a trust is to leave property to a specified person under a will, having extracted a promise from that person to hold the trust property for the benefit of the secret beneficiary. The person named on the face of the will is termed a "secret trustee" or in a fully secret trust, an "ostensible beneficiary". The party who is to receive benefit from the trust is called the "true beneficiary".

A problem arises when the secret trustee seeks to take the property absolute arguing non-compliance with the terms of the Succession Act 1965. In such circumstances, the court may:

(i) abide by the Succession Act 1965 and permit the secret trustee to take the property beneficially;

(ii) order the secret trustee to hold the property on resulting trust for the testator's estate;

(iii) give full effect to the testator's wishes and enforce the secret trust.

The rationale for the recognition of secret trusts is twofold:

(i) The fraud theory—the most common justification for the recognition of secret trusts in that to do otherwise would equate to permitting a statute to be used as vehicle for fraud (see *Re Keen* [1937] 1 All E.R. 452).

(ii) The "*dehors* the will" theory—this provides that due to the fact that a secret trust is not a term of the will, it is therefore not subject to the Succession Act 1965.

FULLY SECRET TRUSTS

In a fully secret trust, the legatee appears, from the face of the will, to be taking the property beneficially under the will. Nothing in the will indicates that he must hold the property on trust for an undisclosed beneficiary, i.e. "€200,000 to Karl".

In the case of *McCormack v Grogan* (1869) LR 4HL 82, Lord Westbury set out three requirements necessary for the existence of a fully secret trust:

(i) there must exist an intention to create a trust;

(ii) there must be communication of the donor's intention to create a trust for the benefit of the donee, during his lifetime; and

(iii) there has to be acceptance on the part of the legatee or secret trustee of the trust obligation.

INTENTION AND COMMUNICATION

If the terms of the secret trust are not communicated to the donee or are only communicated after the death of the testator, the trust will fail. In *Walgrave v Tebbs* [1855] 25 L.J. Ch. 241, it was held that the secret trust failed because the secret trust obligation was not communicated to the donees prior to the death of the testator.

In the case of *Re Boyes* [1884] 32 W.R. 630, Kay J. concluded that in order for a valid secret trust to be upheld, the terms must be communicated to the trustee in the testator's lifetime and the trustee must accept his obligations under the trust. Here, the testator failed to indicate the objects of the trust prior to his death; the trust objects were only discovered after his death. However, Kay J. was of the opinion that:

"It may possibly be that the legatee would be bound if the trust was put in writing and placed in his hands in a sealed envelope, and he had engaged that he would hold that property given to him by the will upon the trust so declared although he did not know the actual terms of the trust."

In *Re Keen* [1937] 1 All E.R. 452, the trust failed as there was an attempt on the part of the testator to define the objects at a later date even though the details of the trust had already been communicated to and accepted by the trustees.

ACCEPTANCE

If a donee fails to accept the trust obligation, he will then hold the property on resulting trust for the testator's estate. Once the donee is aware of the existence of the trust, it is absolute that the donee cannot take the property beneficially.

The court in *Ottaway v Norman* [1971] 3 All E.R. 1325 came to the conclusion that acceptance of obligation under a trust can be implied. In *Moss v Cooper* [1861] 4 L.T. 352, Wood V.C. decided that if the donee, by his silence, led the testator to believe that he had accepted the obligation under the trust, then the court would imply acceptance. The court would not permit his fraudulent behaviour to benefit him.

It is noteworthy that if the testator wishes to make any addition to the trust property, he must comply with the same requirements as have been set out above. A problem arises in circumstances where there is more than one trustee and one or more of them is not informed of the addition to the trust property. Farwell J. in *Re Stead* [1900] 48 W.R. 221 made a distinction between joint tenants and tenants in common. He was of the opinion that where property was transferred to joint tenants and only one legatee accepted the trusts, they would both hold the trust. On the other hand, if property were transferred to tenants in common in the same situation, the trust would only bind the party that undertook the obligation.

Walker L.J. in the case of *Geddis v Semple* [1903] 1 I.R. 73 criticised the decision of Farwell J., emphasising that a tenant in common who was not informed of the existence of a secret trust would not be bound by the undertaking given by his fellow tenant in common.

HALF SECRET TRUSTS

A half secret trust arises where the testator's intention that the donee hold property on trust appears on the face of the will, but the terms of the trust are not specified. Due to their nature, half secret trusts avoid the possibility of fraud.

The historical purpose behind the upholding of a fully secret trust in light of the Succession Act was to prevent fraud. It should be noted that while the English courts have been reluctant to uphold half secret trusts (see in particular, *Blackwell v Blackwell* [1929] A.C. 318), the Irish judiciary has not.

In the Irish case of *Riordan v Bannon* [1876] I.R. 10 Eq. 469, Chatterton V.C., while acknowledging that the same kind of fraud cannot operate in relation to half secret trusts, the refusal to uphold such trusts would be a fraud on the intentions of the settlor.

In *Re Browne* [1944] I.R. 90, Overend J. confirmed that it was immaterial whether or not communication and acceptance took place before or after the execution of the will.

Barron J. in *Prendiville v Prendiville* [1995] 2 I.L.R.M. 578 affirmed the court's decision in *Riordan v Bannon* [1876] I.R. 10 Eq. 469, holding that the half secret trust would be valid in circumstances where there had been communication by the testator and acceptance by the legatee of the terms of the trust during the lifetime of the testator.

PROBLEMS THAT MAY ARISE IN CONNECTION WITH SECRET TRUSTS

ATTESTATION OF THE WILL BY A BENEFICIARY

O'Brien v Condon [1905] 1 I.R. 51 is authority for the fact that a witness to a testamentary instrument will be permitted to benefit under it.

ATTESTATION OF THE WILL BY A LEGATEE

In *Re Armstrong* [1893] 31 L.R. Ir. 154, it was held that a half secret trust was valid where the legatee attested the will.

WHERE A BENEFICIARY PREDECEASES THE TESTATOR

According to the Succession Act 1965, a beneficiary must outlive the testator in order to benefit under the will. However, the case of *Re Gardiner* [1923] 92 L.J. Ch. 569 is a somewhat dubious authority and states that a beneficiary receives his interest as soon as the will is made and the trust is created, rather than when the testator dies.

WHERE THE LEGATEE PREDECEASES THE TESTATOR

Re Maddock [1902] 50 W.R. 598 is authority for the proposition that in a fully secret trust, the legatee's death prior to the death of the testator will cause it to fail. However, with regard to a half secret trust, the death of the legatee prior to the death of the testator will not cause it to fail so long as the purpose of the trust was known.

BENEFICIAL LEGATEES

The Succession Act 1965 does not specifically prevent a legatee from being a beneficiary under a secret trust. However, the courts have taken a cautious view. Pennycuick J. in *Re Pugh* [1887] W.N. 143 was of the opinion that such a situation would raise the suspicion of the court as there would be no useful purpose in creating such a trust.

Purpose Trusts

13

DEFINITION OF A PURPOSE TRUST

Whilst a private trust is in essence a trust in favour of an ascertainable individual, a charitable trust is for a purpose that is treated in law as being charitable. This chapter examines whether or not it is possible to establish a trust with neither an ascertainable individual nor a charitable purpose.

In certain limited circumstances, non-charitable purpose trusts have been upheld. However, the general rule remains that such trusts will fail on the basis that they lack human beneficiaries to enforce them or that they offend the rule against perpetuities/inalienability. However, it should be noted that s.16 of the Land and Conveyancing Law Reform Act 2009 abolished the rule against perpetuities.

THE BENEFICIARY PRINCIPLE

Unlike charitable trusts, the Attorney General cannot enforce a private trust and in order for such a trust to be valid, it must have a human beneficiary by whom the trust can be enforced. Indeed, an objection to non-charitable purpose trusts can be seen in the dicta of Sir William Grant M.R. in the case of *Morice v Bishop of Durham* [1804] 9 Ves. Jr. 399 at 404:

> "Every other trust must have a definite object. There must be somebody in whose favour the court can decree performance."

In *Re Astor's Settlement Trusts* [1952] Ch. 534, a trust for "the maintenance of good understanding between nations and the preservation and integrity of newspapers" was held to be too uncertain as there was no human beneficiary who could police the trust, while the objectives were deemed too abstract and impersonal.

It was noted by Goff J. in *Re Denley's Trust Deed* [1969] 1 Ch. 373 that where a trust is expressed as a purpose trust, but is in fact for the benefit of a person or class of persons, then it may not fail under the beneficiary principle. In essence, the benefit must be worded in such a way as to give any individual locus standi to apply to court to seek to enforce the trust.

PURPOSE TRUSTS

THE REQUIREMENT OF CERTAINTY

It is of the utmost importance for a private trust to be framed in sufficiently clear and certain language so as to enable a court to supervise its performance. In *Morice v Bishop of Durham* [1804] 9 Ves. Jr. 399 at 404, a gift for "such objects of benevolence and liberty as the Bishop of Durham in his own discretion shall most approve of" was held to be invalid by the fact that it lacked sufficient certainty. Indeed, Roxburgh J. in *Re Astor's Settlement Trusts* [1952] Ch. 534 was of the opinion that:

> "If an enumeration of purposes outside the realm of charities can take the place of an enumeration of beneficiaries, the purpose must, in my judgment, be stated in phrases which embody definite concepts and the means by which the trustees are to try to attain them must be prescribed with a sufficient degree of certainty."

In *Re Endacott* [1960] Ch. 232 at 251, the testator bequeathed his residuary estate "for the purpose of providing some useful memorial to myself". Harman L.J. held that this phrase was insufficiently certain and that such a bequest should not be permitted to add to the list of troublesome, anomalous and aberrant cases.

THE RULE AGAINST PERPETUITIES AND INALIENABILITY

The rule against perpetuities and inalienability is based upon public policy, in that it can be said to be contrary to public policy for capital to be tied up for indeterminate and lengthy periods of time. The perpetuity period is a life or lives in being plus 21 years or 21 years only if there is no life in being. It is important to note that before a purpose trust will be enforced, the court has to be satisfied that it will not breach the rule against perpetuities.

A distinction arises between the rule against perpetuities and the rule against inalienability, in that the former is concerned with the time at which the vesting of the interest occurs and the latter is concerned with the duration of the interest that has already vested.

In the case of *Mussett v Bingle* [1876] W.N. 170, a testator gave £300 for the erection of a monument in his honour and a further £200 for its upkeep. Hall V.C. held that the first bequest was valid as it could be carried out within the perpetuity period; however, the maintenance of the monument was infinite and therefore void.

It is important to note that the rule against perpetuities was abolished by s.16 of the Land and Conveyancing Law Reform Act 2009, so a trust will no longer be void ab initio where it might vest outside of the perpetuity period. However, the rule against inalienability persists and so where property is tied to a specific non-charitable purpose, for a period of time in excess of the perpetuity period, the trust will be void.

GIFTS FOR THE CARE OF ANIMALS

In general, trusts for the welfare of animals are deemed to be charitable in nature; however, if a trust is established for the care of a specific animal, it will not be upheld as being a charitable trust. In a concession to human sentiment, despite the absence of a human beneficiary, such trusts have been upheld as being valid purpose trusts.

In *Re Dean* [1889] 41 Ch D 552, a trust for the upkeep of the testator's horses and hounds for a period of 50 years "should they live that long" was held to be valid in the absence of a human beneficiary. It should be noted that this decision is highly irregular, as it sidesteps the issue of perpetuity.

In *Re Kelly* [1932] I.R. 255, a testator left £100 for the purpose of spending £4 per annum for the upkeep of each of his greyhounds, with a gift over if any surplus should remain after the death of the last dog. The gift providing for the maintenance of the dogs was held to be valid as the gift could be severed after 21 years; however, the gift over was void as it offended the rule against perpetuities.

GIFTS TO UNINCORPORATED ASSOCIATIONS

Whilst a gift to a corporation is valid, since it has its own legal personality, a gift to an unincorporated association is void, as it violates the rule against inalienability as property may vest in persons who might join the association at some time in the future. A number of different ways of conferring benefit on unincorporated associations have been developed.

GIFT BY WAY OF ENDOWMENT FOR THE BENEFIT OF THE ASSOCIATION

In general, where a gift is interpreted as an endowment for the benefit of an association, it offends the rule against perpetuities and will be invalid.

GIFTS TO THE MEMBERS OF THE ASSOCIATION FOR THE TIME BEING

It is possible for a gift to an unincorporated association to be upheld in circumstances where the gift is to the members of an association who are alive at the time of the disposition, or in the case of a will, at the date of the testator's death. It is essential that the gift be construed as being for individual members for the time being.

In *Cocks v Manners* [1871] L.R. 12 Eq. 574, a gift that was made to a contemplative order of nuns was upheld as it was treated as a gift to the Mother Superior of the community for the time being.

The Supreme Court in *Re Byrne* [1935] I.R. 782 held that if it was the intention of the testator to divide the gift among individuals forming a class, there could be no objection to the validity of the trust. Murnaghan J. was of the opinion that "the language of the testator must in each case be the guide" and held that a gift of a non-charitable nature for the benefit of an ascertainable class of persons will be upheld.

GIFT TO THE MEMBERS TO BE APPLIED IN ACCORDANCE WITH THEIR CONTRACTUAL RIGHTS AND LIABILITIES

Certain gifts that are subject to the members' contractual rights and liabilities will be upheld. It is important to note that a member cannot sever his share in the gift; it will transfer to others upon his resignation or death.

Brightman J. applied his "contract-holding theory" in *Re Recher's Will Trusts* [1972] Ch. 526, holding that:

> "In the absence of words which purport to impose a trust, the legacy is a gift to the members beneficially, not as joint tenants or as tenants in common so as to entitle each member to an immediate distributive share, but as an accretion to the funds which are the subject matter of the contract which the members have made *inter se*."

A similar approach was adopted by Oliver J. in *Re Lipinski's Will Trusts* [1976] Ch. 235, where he held that the gift in question was valid as an absolute gift to the members beneficially, as an accreditation to its funds, subject to the rules of the association.

MONUMENTS AND TOMBS

Section 50 of the Charities Act 1961 provides that provisions for the maintenance or improvement of tombs, graves, vaults, tombstones or any other memorial to a deceased person are valid charitable trusts once they do not exceed £60 per annum in the case of income and a £1,000 capital sum. As these monetary limits have not been increased since the enactment of the statute, trusts for such purposes in the majority of cases will breach the limits imposed.

In such instances, trusts will only be enforced if they do not offend the rule against inalienability. In *Mussett v Bingle* [1867] W.N. 170, it was held that the courts will assume that trusts for the erection of a monument or tomb will be carried out within the perpetuity period. It is important to note that the trust must also be expressed with sufficient clarity to be carried out.

In *Re Endacott* [1960] Ch. 232 at 251, a bequest was made "for the purpose of providing some useful memorial to myself". Harman L.J. held that the gift was void stating that "I cannot think a case of this kind, the case of providing outside a church an unspecified and unidentified memorial, is the kind of instance which should be allowed to add to those troublesome, anomalous and abberrant cases". A gift for the maintenance of a memorial will be invalid unless accompanied with sufficient words of qualification.

14 Charitable Trusts

INTRODUCTION

Although the Charities Act 2009 came into effect in February 2009, it is important to note that very few of its sections have been commenced (ss.1, 2, 5, 10(1) and (2) and 99 came into effect as a result of the Charities Act 2009 (Commencement) Order 2009 (S.I. No. 284 of 2009); ss.4 and 90 came into effect as a result of the Charities Act 2009 (Commencement Order) 2010 (S.I. No. 315 of 2010)). Pursuant to s.13 a new regulatory framework will be established under a Charities Regulatory Authority, which will take over the functions currently exercised by both the Attorney General and the Commissioners of Charitable Donations and Bequests. The new Charities Regulatory Authority will possess extensive powers in order to regulate the administration of charitable trusts.

CLASSIFICATION

Charitable trusts are public in nature and are intended to promote a purpose that is beneficial to society. They are an exception to the general rule that, before a trust can be valid, it must have human objects.

The Irish Statute of Charitable Uses 1634 governed the creation of charitable trusts, with its Preamble stipulating what objects might be deemed as charitable. The Preamble was relied upon until it was repealed by the Statute Law Revision Act (Ireland) 1878. However, it is useful to set out the terms of the Preamble as it gives an insight into the question of what is classed as charitable:

> "[T]he erection, maintenance, or support of any college, schoole, lecture in divinity or in any of the liberal arts or science; or for the reliefe, of any manner of poore, succourlesse, distressed, or impotent persons; or for the building, re-edifying, or maintaining in repaire any church, college, schoole or hospital; or for the errection, building, maintenance, or repair of any bridges, causeyes, cashes, paces and highways within this realme; or for any other like lawfull and charitable use and uses, warranted by the laws of this realme now established and in force ..."

The authoritative classification of charitable trusts was identified by Lord Macnaghten in *Commissioners for Special Purposes of Income Tax v Pemsel* [1891] A.C. 531:

    (i) trusts for the relief of poverty;
    (ii) trusts for the advancement of education;
    (iii) trusts for the advancement of religion; and
    (iv) trusts for other purposes beneficial to the community.

This classification fails to make clear that in order for a trust to be charitable, there must exist some element of benefit to the public. Section 3(4) of the Charities Act 2009 provides that "it shall be presumed, unless the contrary is proved, that a gift for the advancement of religion will occasion public benefit". This is broadly in line with s.45(1) of the Charities Act 1961 which went further and provided that it shall be conclusively presumed that a trust for the advancement of religion will occasion public benefit.

Some consideration was also given to the meaning of the concept of "public benefit" (which is preserved in a similar manner by s.3 of the Charities Act 2006 in England) by Briggs J. in *Catholic Care (Diocese of Leeds) v Charity Commission of England and Wales* [2010] EWHC 520 (Ch.) at para.67. He stated that s.3 expressly contemplates that purposes commonly regarded as charitable, such as the advancement of religion or education or the relief of sickness or poverty, may not be for the public benefit, for example if it is sought to achieve these purposes in a particular manner. He added that: "[I]t therefore admits of the possibility that the question whether a particular purpose which is within section 2(2) is charitable may require a weighing of the public benefits and dis-benefits associated with its implementation."

In *Cp. Bath & North Eastern Somerset Council v Attorney General* [2002] EWCA 1623, Hart J. stated that if a trust is to succeed under the fourth *Pemsel* category, then:

> "First, the purpose itself must be beneficial as one of public utility; and secondly, the benefit of the purpose must be available to a sufficient section of the community."

There are a number of advantages associated with charitable status:

    (i) **Enforceability**—Charitable trusts do not require ascertainable beneficiaries in order to enforce them.
    (ii) **Certainty**—Provided that the objects of the trust are wholly and exclusively charitable, it will not fail for lack of specificity in choosing a charitable cause. Also, there is no requirement for human objects.

(iii) **Perpetuity**—Charitable trusts need not be limited in perpetuity. Provided that the gift vests in a charity within the perpetuity period, a gift over to another charity may occur outside this period. As a charity is not subject to the rule against inalienability, capital may be tied up for an indefinite period.

(iv) **Fiscal advantages**—There exist many fiscal advantages associated with charitable status, with the most important being the privileged tax position that it attracts.

TRUSTS FOR THE RELIEF OF POVERTY

"Trusts for the relief of poverty" will be modified to "the prevention or relief of poverty or economic hardship" by s.3 of the Charities Act 2009 and therefore, existing case law will have to be read in light of s.3(7) and (8) of the 2009 Act. Section 3 states:

(1) For the purposes of this Act each of the following shall, subject to *subsection (2)*, be a charitable purpose:
   (*a*) the prevention or relief of poverty or economic hardship;
   (*b*) the advancement of education;
   (*c*) the advancement of religion;
   (*d*) any other purpose that is of benefit to the community.

Over the years, "poverty" has been given a reasonably broad definition in the case law that has developed around the Preamble of the Irish Statute of Charitable Uses 1634. It is by no means necessary for a person to be destitute in order for a trust to be classified as charitable. In *Re Coulthurst* [1951] Ch. 661 at 665–666, the court stated that:

"It is quite clearly established that poverty does not mean destitution; it is a word of wide and somewhat indefinite import; it may not unfairly be paraphrased for present purposes as meaning persons who have to 'go short' in the ordinary acceptation of that term, due regard being had to their status in life, and so forth."

Modern case law signals a more flexible approach to the degree of poverty that must be established. In *Re Segelman Deceased* [1996] Ch. 171 at 190, Chadwick J. held that a gift to the poor and needy members of the testator's relatives was a valid charitable trust for the relief of poverty. It was noted that "most members of the class are comfortably off, in the sense that they are able to meet their day-to-day expenses out of their income, but are not affluent", and "like many others in similar circumstances, they need a helping hand from time to time in order to overcome an unforeseen crises".

It should be noted that a gift must be for the relief of poverty and a gift to entertain the poor would not be upheld. In *Baddeley v IRC* [1953] 1 W.L.R. 84, Harman J. ruled that a gift to amuse the poor would not relieve them from poverty and therefore would not be considered charitable in nature.

In general, in order for a trust to be deemed to be charitable, there must be some degree of public benefit. Therefore, gifts to specified poor individuals rather than to a class of the poor are not valid charitable trusts. In *Re Compton* [1945] Ch. 123 at 131, Lord Greene was of the opinion that "a gift under which the beneficiaries are defined by reference to a purely personal relationship to a named *propositus*, cannot on principle be a valid charitable gift".

However, an exception exists to this general principle and was put in the following terms by Evershed M.R. in *Re Scarisbrick* [1951] Ch. 622 at 639:

> "The 'poor relations' cases may be justified on the basis that the relief of poverty is of so altruistic a character that the public element may necessarily be inferred thereby; or may be accepted as a hallowed, if illogical, exception."

It was further stated at 649 that:

> "The exception operates whether the personal tie is one of blood (as in the numerous so called 'poor relations' cases) or of contract, e.g., the relief of poverty amongst the members of a particular society … or amongst employees of a particular company or their dependants."

The relaxing of the public benefit requirement has been extended to include the establishment of charitable trusts for poor members (see *Re Young* [1955] 1 W.L.R. 1269, where a trust for members of a social club was held to be charitable in nature) and poor employees. The House of Lords decision in *Dingle v Turner* [1972] A.C. 601 at 623, confirmed that trusts for the benefit of poor employees will be recognised as valid charitable trusts. Lord Cross of Chelsea held that:

> "But the 'poor members' and the 'poor employees' decisions were a natural development of the 'poor relations' decisions and to draw a distinction between different sorts of 'poverty' trusts would be quite illogical and could certainly not be said to be introducing 'greater harmony' into the law of charity. Moreover, though not as old as the

'poor relations' trusts 'poor employees' trusts have been recognised as charities for many years; there are now a large number of such trusts in existence; and assuming, as one must, that they are properly administered in the sense that benefits under them are only given to people who can fairly be said to be, according to current standards, 'poor persons', to treat such trusts as charities is not open to any practical objection."

The principle as laid down by Lord Cross has been extended to include poor members of a profession. In *Re Denison* [1974] 42 D.L.R. (3d) 652, the High Court of Ontario ruled that a bequest that provided for the relief of poverty amongst "impoverished or indigent members of the Law Society and of wives and widows and children" was charitable.

TRUSTS FOR THE ADVANCEMENT OF EDUCATION

Mention is made to the maintenance of schools of learning, free schools and university scholars in the Preamble to the Irish Statute of Charitable Uses 1634. Trusts for the advancement of education have long been recognised as being charitable in nature and s.3(1)(b) of the Charities Act 2009 expressly provides that the advancement of education is a charitable purpose.

Over the years, case law has primarily concerned itself with the question as to what constitutes "education". In *Re Shaw* [1957] 1 W.L.R. 729, Harman J. took a rather narrow approach to what constitutes education. Here, George Bernard Shaw left a legacy which provided for research to be carried out into the advantages of the reform of the alphabet. Harman J. took the view that "if the object be merely the increase of knowledge that is not in itself a charitable object unless it be combined with teaching or education."

A more unrestrained approach was taken as to the meaning of "education" in the case of *Re Hopkins' Will Trusts* [1965] Ch. 669 at 680, where Wilberforce J. was of the opinion that the discovery of the original Bacon-Shakespere Manuscripts would be of value to literature, stating:

"I think, therefore, that the word 'education' as used by Harman J in *Re Shaw* must be used in a wide sense, certainly extending beyond teaching, and that the requirement is that, in order to be charitable, research must either be of educational value to the researcher or must be directed as to lead to something which will pass into the store of educational material, or so as to improve the sum of communicable knowledge in an area which education may cover—education in this last context extending to the formation of literary taste and appreciation."

This interpretation, that in order for "education" to be deemed charitable in nature it must be more than an accumulation of knowledge and must involve some element of publication, was adopted by the Court of Appeal in *Incorporated Council for Law Reporting for England and Wales v Attorney General* [1972] Ch. 73 at 102. Buckley L.J. stated that the advancement of education as being a valid charitable purpose must extend "to the improvement of a useful branch of human knowledge and its public dissemination".

A liberal approach to the question of what constitutes "education" can be seen in the judgment of Keane J. in *Re Worth Library* [1995] 2 I.R. 301 at 337. Indeed in his judgment, Keane J. was more drawn towards the reasoning of Buckley L.J. in *Incorporated Council for Law Reporting for England and Wales v Attorney General* than Harman J. in *Re Shaw*. This case concerned a proposed cy-près scheme in relation to a bequest made by Dr Worth of his library to the trustees of Dr Steven's Hospital in Dublin. It was held that the initial bequest was for the advancement of education, with Keane J. stating that:

> "... [G]ifts for the advancement of education ... would embrace, not merely gifts to schools and universities and the endowment of university chairs and scholarships: 'education' has been given a broad meaning so as to encompass gifts for the establishment of theatres, art galleries and museums and the promotion of literature and music. In every case, however, the element of public benefit must be present and, if the benefit extends to a section of the community only, the section must not be numerically negligible."

TRUSTS FOR THE ADVANCEMENT OF RELIGION

Trusts of this nature were identified in the Preamble to the Irish Statute of Charitable Uses 1634. There exists a distinct divergence between Irish and English law on the subject, with the English courts applying an objective approach and the Irish courts applying a more subjective approach. This subjective approach has been given statutory recognition in the form of s.45 of the Charities Act 1961, which provides that:

(1) In determining whether or not a gift for the purpose of the advance-ment of religion is a valid charitable gift it shall be conclusively presumed that the purpose includes and will occasion public benefit.
(2) For the avoidance of the difficulties which arise in giving effect to the intentions of donors of certain gifts for the purpose of

the advancement of religion and in order not to frustrate those intentions and notwithstanding that certain gifts for the purpose aforesaid, including gifts for the celebration of Masses, whether in public or in private, are valid charitable gifts, it is hereby enacted that a valid charitable gift for the purpose of the advancement of religion shall have effect and, as respects its having effect, shall be construed in accordance with the laws, canons, ordinances and tenets of the religion concerned."

It is important to note that s.3(4) of the Charities Act 2009 provides that "[i]t shall be presumed, unless the contrary is proved, that a gift for the advancement of religion is of public benefit". Furthermore, s.3(5) provides that the Charities Regulatory Authority shall not make a determination that a gift for the advancement of religion is not of public benefit without the consent of the Attorney General.

Section 3(10) places a limit on what may be treated as a gift for the advancement of religion:

> if it is made to or for the benefit of an organisation or cult—
> *(a)* the principal object of which is the making of profit, or
> *(b)* that employs oppressive psychological manipulation—
>   (i) of its followers, or
>   (ii) for the purpose of gaining new followers.

In *Arnott v Arnott (No. 2)* [1906] 1 I.R. 127 at 134, O'Connor M.R. held that "a gift for religious purposes and not more will be construed by the court as confined to such religious purposes as are in their nature charitable". In any event, for a trust to be charitable, it must be for the advancement of religion and according to the court in *Keren Kayemeth Le Jisroel v IRC* [1931] 2 K.B. 65, this means:

> "... the promotion of spiritual teaching in a wide sense and the maintenance of the doctrines on which this rests, and the observances that serve to promote and manifest it—not merely a foundation or cause to which it can be related."

GIFTS FOR THE CELEBRATION OF MASSES

The question of whether or not a gift for the celebration of masses is a valid charitable trust for the advancement of religion was addressed by the court in *Commissioners of Charitable Donations and Bequests v Walsh* [1828] 7 Ir.

Eq. R. 34n, with Lord Manners L.C. confirming the charitable status of such a gift.

The English position is that for a gift for the celebration of masses to be a valid charitable trust, the masses must be held in public. Browne-Wilkinson V.C. confirmed this in the case of *Re Hetherington* [1989] 2 W.L.R. 1094, indicating that in order for the public element to be satisfied, the celebration of masses must not be held in private. On the contrary, the Court of Appeal in *O'Hanlon v Logue* [1906] 1 I.R. 247 held that a gift for the saying of masses would be upheld, whether or not the masses be celebrated publicly or privately.

Section 45(2) of the Charities Act 1961 confirms that gifts for the celebration of masses are valid charitable trusts.

GIFTS TO RELIGIOUS ORDERS

Historically, the case law has sought to distinguish gifts to religious orders on the basis that they are contemplative orders, in that they failed to fulfil the necessary public benefit requirement. This point is illustrated by the case of *Cocks v Manners* [1871] L.R. 12 Eq. 574. Wickens V.C., whilst holding that a gift to the Sisters of Charity was a valid charitable trust because it was a "voluntary association for the purpose of teaching the ignorant and nursing the sick", determined that a gift to a Dominican convent was not charitable in nature as it had "none of the requisites of a charitable institution".

The position as regards gifts to contemplative orders was made clear in *Commissioners of Charitable Donations and Bequests v McCartan* [1917] 1 I.R. 388 at 396, with O'Connor M.R. stating that:

> "Monasteries of men and women are often, if not mostly, institutions, the members of which devote their lives exclusively to acts of piety such as pious meditation, prayer and self denial. Such institutions, however praiseworthy, are not charitable in the sense recognised by this Court."

Gavin Duffy J. in *Maguire v Attorney General* [1943] I.R. 238 at 248–249 questioned the view that contemplative religious orders failed to provide the public with the benefit necessary for a charitable trust:

> "I shall waste no time in establishing the proposition of fact that the cloister is a powerful source of general edification in this country. The finding, or assumption, in *Cocks v Manners* that the convent of a contemplative community tended neither directly nor indirectly towards public edification has no scintilla of authority as a determinant of the actual position among us."

Gifts to ecclesiastical office holders

It appears from the case law that whilst a gift to an individual holding ecclesiastical office is not regarded as being charitable, a gift to the holder of such an office for the time being is regarded as charitable. In *Donnellan v O'Neill* [1870] I.R. 5 Eq. 523, a gift to a bishop absolutely for his own use was held not to be charitable in nature. On the other hand, in *Gibson v Representative Church Body* [1881] 9 L.R. Ir. 1, a bequest to the holder of the office of Chaplain in the Rotunda Hospital and all subsequent successors was held to be charitable.

Note should be taken of s.49(1) of the Charities Act 1961:

> Where any of the purposes of a gift includes or could be deemed to include both charitable and non-charitable objects, its terms shall be so construed and given effect to as to exclude the non-charitable objects and the purpose shall, accordingly, be treated as charitable.

Gifts for churches, monuments, tombs, etc

Gifts for the upkeep and repair of a churchyard or cemetery will be regarded as being charitable in nature (see *Re Vaughan* [1886] 33 Ch D 187). Section 50 of the Charities Act 1961 provides that:

> (1) Every gift made after the commencement of this Act for the provision, maintenance or improvement of a tomb, vault or grave or of a tombstone or any other memorial to a deceased person or deceased persons which would not otherwise be charitable shall, to the extent provided by this section, be a charitable gift.
> (2) Such a gift shall, be charitable so far as it does not exceed—
>   (*a*) in the case of a gift of income only, sixty pounds a year,
>   (*b*) in any other case, one thousand pounds in amount or value.

Trusts for other purposes beneficial to the community

This fourth head of charity represents a hotchpotch of worthy causes which have been recognised as being charitable in nature. Section 3 of the Charities Act 2009 sets out a non-exhaustive list by stating that the phrase "purpose that is of benefit to the community" includes—

(*a*) the advancement of community welfare including the relief of those in need by reason of youth, age, ill-health or disability,
(*b*) the advancement of community development, including rural or urban regeneration,

(c) the promotion of civic responsibility or voluntary work,
(d) the promotion of health, including the prevention or relief of sickness, disease or human suffering,
(e) the advancement of conflict resolution or reconciliation,
(f) the promotion of religious or racial harmony and harmonious community relations,
(g) the protection of the natural environment,
(h) the advancement of environmental sustainability,
(i) the advancement of the efficient and effective use of the property of charitable organisations,
(j) the prevention or relief of suffering of animals,
(k) the advancement of the arts, culture, heritage or sciences, and
(l) the integration of those who are disadvantaged, and the promotion of their full participation, in society.

It is important to note that the absence of a purpose from the above list does not mean that it cannot be considered as being charitable, unless it falls within the scope of an "excluded body" as defined in s.2 of the 2009 Act.

This category is not as straightforward as the other heads of charity, as not every purpose beneficial to the community will be held to be charitable. Indeed, this view was developed by Viscount Cave in *Attorney General v National Provincial and Union Bank of England Ltd* [1924] A.C. 262 at 265:

> "Lord Macnaghten did not mean that all trusts for purposes beneficial to the community are charitable, but that there were certain charitable trusts which fell within that category; and accordingly to argue that because a trust is for a purpose beneficial to the community it is therefore a charitable trust is to turn round his sentence and to give it a different meaning. So here it is not enough to say that the trust in question is for the public purposes beneficial to the community or for the public welfare; you must also show it to be a charitable trust."

More recently, an innovative flexible approach was taken to the dicta of Lord McNaghten in *Incorporated Council for Law reporting for England and Wales v AG* [1972] Ch. 73, with Russell L.J. noting that if the purpose of the trust is of sufficient benefit to the community, it is prima facie charitable in law.

Whilst the courts of England and Wales take an objective approach to public benefit (see *Re Hummeltenberg* [1923] 1 Ch. 237), the Irish courts seem to have adopted a more subjective approach. In adopting the decision of the Court of Appeal in *Re Cranston* [1898] 1 I.R. 431, Keane J. in *Re Worth Library* [1995] 2 I.R. 301 at 335 stated:

"In every case, the intention of the testator is of paramount importance. If he intended to advance a charitable object recognised as such by the law, his gift will be a charitable gift. In the case of gifts which do not come within the first three categories, the fact that the testator's view as to the public utility of his favoured object—e.g. vegetarianism—is not shared by many people will not in itself prevent it from being, in the eyes of the law, a valid charitable object within the fourth category, provided it is not illegal, irrational or *contra bonos mores*. That, as I understand is the effect of the majority decision of the Irish Courts of Appeal *In Re Cranston*."

At this point it is useful to consider a number of purposes which have traditionally been considered as being charitable.

GIFTS FOR THE UPKEEP OF ANIMALS

Generally, trusts for the welfare of animals are deemed to be charitable in nature. However, if a trust is established for the care of a specific animal, it will not be held as being a charitable trust. In a concession to human sentiment, despite the absence of a human beneficiary, such trusts have been upheld as valid purpose trusts. Section 3(11)(j) of the Charities Act 2009 now specifically includes trusts for "the prevention or relief of suffering of animals".

In *Re Kelly* [1932] I.R. 255, a testator left £100 for the purpose of spending £4 per annum for the upkeep of each of his greyhounds, with a gift over if any surplus should remain after the death of the last dog. The gift providing for the maintenance of the dogs was held to be valid as the gift could be severed after 21 years; however, the gift over was void as it offended the rule against perpetuities.

In *Maguire v Attorney General* [1943] I.R. 238, Gavin Duffy J. was of the opinion that such trusts were indeed charitable in nature as kindness towards animals should be promoted for the benefit of the community.

Some English case law suggests that the validity of gifts in favour of animals is dependent upon whether or not it results in any benefit to mankind. In *Re Grove Grady* [1929] 1 Ch. 557, it was held that a trust merely for the benefit of animals was not charitable.

In *National Anti-Vivisection Society v Inland Revenue Commissioners* [1948] A.C. 31, the House of Lords refused to accept that the plaintiff society had charitable status in circumstances where it was accepted that whilst the protection of animals from cruelty was a charitable purpose, vivisection was a necessary medical research tool and so of benefit to the public. This point was reiterated by Buckley J. in *Re Jenkin's Will Trusts* [1966] Ch. 249 at 255:

"[T]he prohibiting of any forms of cruelty inherent in vivisection, however admirable that may be from an ethical point of view, is not a charitable activity in the contemplation of the law because the court cannot weigh the benefits to the community which result from using animals for vivisection and research against the benefits which would result to the community from preventing such practices."

It was held by Lewison J. in *Hanchett-Stamford v Attorney-General* [2009] Ch. 173 that the Performing and Captive Animal Defence League was not a charitable trust. While he accepted that a trust which had as its sole object the prevention of cruelty to performing animals would be capable of being charitable, as one of the objects of the league was to secure an outright ban on performing animals, which would involve a change in the law, he concluded that its purpose was not charitable in nature.

GIFTS FOR THE AGED, THE DISABLED AND THE SICK

Although trusts as defined by the Irish Statute of Charitable Uses 1634 "for the reliefe of any manner of poore, succourlesse, distressed, or impotent persons" have historically been legally charitable, s.3(11) of the Charities Act 2009 provides that a purpose that is of benefit to the community includes "the promotion of health, including the prevention or relief of sickness, disease or human suffering" amongst those in need by reason of youth, age, ill-health or sickness.

In the case of *Re McCarthy's Will Trusts* [1958] I.R. 311, Budd J. held that trusts for the benefit of the sick were clearly charitable in nature. In *Barrington's Hospital v Valuation Commissioner* [1957] I.R. 299, Kingsmill Moore J. was of the opinion that a trust for the care of the sick or upkeep of a hospital should be recognised as being a valid charitable trust.

Furthermore, Keane J. in *Re Worth Library* [1995] 2 I.R. 301, in relying on *Re McCarthy's Will Trusts*, held that a gift for the benefit of a hospital was charitable in nature.

It should be noted that in *Odstock Private Care Ltd's Application for Registration as a Charity* [2008] W.T.L.R. 675, the Charity Commissioners held that a company which provided private health care at an NHS hospital could not be registered as a charity where its services were not available to the public at large, because those living in poverty could not afford the fees.

GIFTS FOR SPORTING AND RECREATIONAL PURPOSES

Historically, whilst trusts providing for recreation facilities have been upheld as being charitable, trusts for the promotion of individual sports have not. In *Re Nottage* [1895] 2 Ch. 649, the English Court of Appeal refused to uphold a gift for the purpose of encouraging yacht racing as being charitable, noting that gifts merely to encourage sports were not charitable in nature.

The Charities Act 2009 does not make any reference to the advancement of any form of sporting activity in the list of purposes contained within s.3. In fact s.2 defines "excluded body" as being an approved body within the meaning of s.235 of the Taxes Consolidation Act 1997, which is "any body of persons established for and existing for the sole purpose of promoting athletic or amateur games or sports".

Both recent case law and legislative provisions made it clear that the advancement of amateur sport will not qualify as a legally charitable purpose in this jurisdiction. This issue was considered by Charleton J. in *National Tourism Development Authority v Coughlan* [2009] IEHC 53, in which he had to consider whether a trust, the subject matter of which was golf courses, could be charitable in nature. In summarising his observations on the issues raised Charleton J. stated at para.19, inter alia, as follows:

> "Sport has never been recognised to be an object of sufficiently wide benefit to the community as to enjoy charitable status. The law has traditionally regarded sport as a form of recreation and, in consequence, trusts and bequests for sporting purposes are not recognised as charitable."

GIFTS FOR POLITICAL PURPOSES

It is widely accepted that gifts for political purposes are not charitable. This principle was highlighted in this jurisdiction in the case of *Re Ní Brudair*, unreported, High Court, Gannon J., February 5, 1979.

In *McGovern v Attorney General* [1982] Ch. 321 at 340, Slade J. lay down the following principles:

> "Trusts for political purposes ... include (*inter alia*) trusts of which a direct and principal purpose is either—(i) to further the interests of a particular political party, or (ii) to procure changes in the laws of this country, or (iii) to procure changes in the laws of a foreign country, or (iv) to procure a reversal of government policy or of particular decisions of governmental authorities in this country, or (v) to procure a reversal of government policy or of particular decisions of governmental authorities in a foreign country."

Indeed, s.2(1) of the Charities Act 2009 provides that a charitable organisation shall not include an "excluded body" which is defined to include:

(a) a political party, or a body that promotes a political party or candidate or

(b) a body that promotes a political cause, unless the promotion of that cause relates directly to the advancement of the charitable purposes of that body.

CY-PRÈS JURISDICTION

In certain circumstances, where a gift is made for a charitable purpose and that purpose cannot be carried out in the precise manner intended by the donor, the cy-près doctrine permits a court to make a scheme for the application of the property for another charitable purpose that is as close to the donor's intentions as possible. The courts have an inherent jurisdiction as well as a statutory obligation under s.47 of the Charities Act 1961 (see below) to invoke the cy-près jurisdiction. In the case of *Re Worth Library* [1995] 2 I.R. 301, Keane J. suggested that in order for the cy-près jurisdiction to be applied, the court must first satisfy itself that the bequest is charitable in nature.

Meredith J. in *Governors of Erasmus Smith's Schools v Attorney General* [1931] 66 I.L.T.R. 57 at 61 described the function of the doctrine of cy-près as follows:

> "To apply without modification a charitable intention that is only expressed in relation to assumed facts and under different conditions is obviously not to carry out the real intention at all. It is on this principle that Courts of Law adapt the statement of a charitable intention to suit altered circumstances and conditions with a view to giving effect to the real intention. Donors cannot be expected to provide expressly for more than the world and the times with which they are familiar."

A distinction is drawn between (i) the initial failure of a charitable purpose and (ii) supervening impossibility.

FAILURE OF CHARITABLE PURPOSE

In circumstances where the charitable purpose of a gift fails, the doctrine of cy-près may be applied "where in form, the gift is given for a particular charitable purpose, but it is possible taking the will as a whole, to say that, notwithstanding the form of the gift, the paramount intention, according to the true construction of the will, is to give the property in the first instance for a general charitable purpose rather than a particular charitable purpose ..." as per Parker J. in *Re Wilson* [1913] 1 Ch. 314 at 320–321.

The courts tend to take a liberal view, thus not allowing a prima facie charitable gift to fail. In *Re Prescott* [1990] 2 I.R. 342, the deceased left her property to "the Holy Protection Parish Dublin of the Russian Orthodox Church abroad" and stipulated that it be sold "if and when there are no parishoners or members of the said church living in Ireland". It subsequently came to light that the Parish had been dissolved prior to her death and no member of the clergy of the church resided in Ireland. MacKenzie J. held that a general charitable intention could be determined from a single gift; however, in these circumstances, the testatrix failed to indicate that it was her intention to benefit anyone other than the named institution and so the court refused to apply its cy-près jurisdiction.

The cy-près jurisdiction of the courts has been applied in circumstances where the intended beneficiary refuses to accept the gift on the terms upon which it is made. In *Re Dunwoodie* [1977] N.I. 141, the court held that a gift for the installation of bells in a church, in circumstances where the Parish Council had decided not to install the bells, could be applied for other religious purposes as there existed a general intention on the part of the testatrix to advance religion.

Supervening impossibility

It is not necessary to establish a general charitable intention if the gift is given absolutely and perpetually to charity. In *Re Royal Hospital Kilmainham* [1966] I.R. 451 at 469, Budd J. noted that:

> "... the cy-près principle is confined, however, to cases where property is given with a general intention to charity with this exception, that where the property is given absolutely and perpetually to charity for a particular purpose and has vested in the charity the fund can be applied cy-près irrespective of the donor's particular intention."

In *Re Worth Library* [1995] 2 I.R. 301, Keane J. held that where there has been an absolute and perpetual gift to charity, cy-près jurisdiction should be applied.

The provisions of s.47(1) of the Charities Act 1961 were applied by O'Hanlon J. in *Representative Church Body v Attorney General* [1988] I.R. 19 and the decision illustrates the relaxation of the original common law requirements of cy-près jurisdiction. The court held that as the original purposes of the gift had ceased to provide an effective method of using the property that was available, the property could be sold and applied to another purpose.

(1) Subject to subsection (2), the circumstances in which the original purposes of a charitable gift may be altered to allow the property given or part of it to be applied *cy-prés* shall be as follows:—

(a) where the original purposes, in whole or in part—
  (i) have been as far as may be fulfilled; or
  (ii) cannot be carried out, or cannot be carried out according to the directions given and to the spirit of the gift; or

(b) where the original purposes provide a use for part only of the property available by virtue of the gift; or

(c) where the property available by virtue of the gift and other property applicable for similar purposes can be more effectively used in conjunction, and to that end can suitably, regard being had to the spirit of the gift, be made applicable to common purposes; or

(d) where the original purposes were laid down by reference to an area which then was, but has since ceased to be a unit for some other purpose, or by reference to a class of persons or to an area which has for any reason since ceased, either to be suitable, regard being had to the spirit of the gift, or to be practical in administering the gift; or

(e) where the original purposes, in whole or in part, have, since they were laid down—
  (i) been adequately provided for by other means; or
  (ii) ceased, as being useless or harmful to the community or for other reasons, to be in law charitable; or
  (iii) ceased in any other way to provide a suitable and effective method of using the property available by virtue of the gift, regard being had to the spirit of the gift.

(2) Subsection (1) shall not affect the conditions which must be satisfied in order that property given for charitable purposes may be applied *cy-près*, except in so far as those conditions require a failure of the original purposes.

(3) References in the foregoing subsections to the original purposes of a gift shall be construed, where the application of the property given has been altered or regulated by a scheme or otherwise, as referring to the purposes for which the property is for the time being applicable.

(4) It is hereby declared that a trust for charitable purposes places a trustee under a duty, where the case permits and requires the property or some part of it to be applied *cy-près*, to secure its effective use for charity by taking steps to enable it to be so applied.

(5) This section shall apply to property given for charitable purposes, notwithstanding that it was so given before the commencement of this Act.

15 Void and Voidable Trusts

INTRODUCTION

A perfectly valid private trust may not be upheld in circumstances where it is held to be contrary to public policy or, in fact, illegal. Trusts that are contrary to public policy or illegal are void ab initio, in that they are deemed to have never come into effect. On the other hand, trusts that are merely voidable will remain in force until such time as their validity is undermined.

At this point it is important to distinguish between conditions precedent and conditions subsequent as it more often than not relates to the condition of validity of a trust. A condition precedent will prevent a trust from coming into existence until a specified condition is satisfied. A condition subsequent does not prevent the trust from coming into force, but may render it liable to divestment if a specified act occurs.

It is noteworthy that where real property is held on trust subject to a condition precedent, the trust will fail in its entirety if the condition is held to be void.

VOID TRUSTS

TRUSTS IN RESTRAINT OF MARRIAGE

Having regard to the right to marry as an unenumerated right under Art.40.3 of the Constitution, any trust which attempts to restrain marriage is clearly void. However, in the case of *Allen v Jackson* [1875] 1 Ch D 399, it was made clear by Mellish L.J. that restrictions on marriage will not void a trust in circumstances where they are intended only to take effect upon the happening of a second marriage.

In *Re Johnson's Will Trusts* [1967] Ch. 387, a trust that reduced the beneficiary's interest so long as she remained married to her husband was held to be void. This can be distinguished from the decision in *Re Lovell* [1920] 1 Ch. 122, where the object of a trust that made provision for a woman during her separation in circumstances where she was already separated was held to be valid. It is unlikely that any provision which directly or indirectly weakens the bond of marriage in light of the Constitution would be upheld in this jurisdiction.

TRUSTS THAT INTERFERE WITH PARENTAL RIGHTS

Trusts that result in the weakening of the bond between parent and child have been held to be contrary to public policy and thus void.

In *Re Boulter* [1922] 1 Ch. 75, a trust was established by the testator for the purpose of maintaining his grandchildren for as long as they resided in England and were not residing abroad. The trust was held to be void as it tended to encourage the separation of parents from their children. Further, trusts that interfere with parental rights and duties have been held to be void (see *Re Borwick* [1933] Ch. 657).

Conditions that tend to interfere with parental rights in relation to education have rarely been upheld. In *Re Burke's Estate* [1951] I.R. 216, a trust was set up for the education of an infant, by requiring him to receive a Roman Catholic education. Gavin Duffy P. held that the condition tended to interfere with the rights of parents to educate their children in light of Art.42 of the Constitution. The court also drew a distinction between invalidity of trusts in relation to conditions precedent and conditions subsequent at 224:

> "The practical effect of the distinction is of the utmost importance: a gift made subject to a condition precedent fails altogether, as a rule, if the condition is found to be void, but if a gift is made subject to a condition subsequent which is found to be void or inapplicable, the condition disappears and the gift takes effect independently of the condition."

The decision in *Re Doyle*, unreported, High Court, Kenny J., 1972, seems to suggest that where a condition, even a condition precedent, is attached to a trust and it violates a constitutional right, then the donee takes absolutely without being bound by the condition.

VOIDABLE TRUSTS

Unlike a void trust, a trust that is voidable remains in being until a court sets it aside. A trust may be voidable in a number of ways, including fraud, misrepresentation, mistake, undue influence and duress. We are concerned here with the statutory intervention which has prescribed that certain trusts be set aside.

VOLUNTARY SETTLEMENTS TO DEFRAUD PURCHASERS

Section 1 of the Conveyancing Act (Ireland) 1634 (the "1634 Act") originally provided that any voluntary conveyance made with the intention of defrauding subsequent purchasers is void as against subsequent purchasers for value.

Section 3 excludes bona fide conveyances for good consideration from the ambit of s.1. However, ss.74(1) and (2) of the Land and Conveyancing Law Reform Act 2009 have repealed s.1 of the 1634 Act. Subsection 1 provides that "[s]ubject to *subsection (2)*, any voluntary disposition of land made with the intention of defrauding a subsequent purchaser of the land is voidable by that purchaser", with subs.2 providing that:

> [F]or the purposes of *subsection (1)*, a voluntary disposition is not to be read as intended to defraud merely because a subsequent disposition of the same land was made for valuable consideration.

Hamilton P. in *Re O'Neill* [1989] I.R. 544 defined "bona fide" in the context of the 1634 Act as being "without notice of the intention to delay, hinder or defraud creditors of their lawful debts, rights and remedies". In *Gardiner v Gardiner* [1861] 12 I.C.L.R. 565, Monahan C.J. stated that:

> "[F]rom the fact of the deed being voluntary, we are justified in drawing the inference that the deed was made with the intent to defraud purchasers."

In response to this harsh presumption of fraud, which operated to invalidate many bona fide family settlements, the Voluntary Conveyances Act 1893 was passed. Section 2 of the Act provides that a voluntary conveyance which is made bona fide and without any fraudulent intent should not be irrebuttably deemed to be fraudulent within the meaning of the earlier statute.

In *National Bank Ltd v Behan* [1913] 1 I.R. 512, O'Connor M.R. was of the opinion that the onus of proving the bona fides of a voluntary conveyance fell firmly at the feet of the person seeking to uphold the conveyance.

The court in *Moore v Kelly* [1918] 1 I.R. 169 was of the view that the onus lay on the party seeking to impugn the deed, with O'Brien L.C. stating at 179 that "where an actual intent to defraud the grantor's creditors is alleged, the burden of proving such intent falls on the person alleging it".

SETTLEMENTS BY BANKRUPTS

Section 59 of the Bankruptcy Act 1988 (the "1988 Act") provides for the setting aside of certain settlements made by persons who subsequently become bankrupt:

> (1) Any settlement of property, not being a settlement made before and in consideration of marriage, or made in favour of a purchaser or incumbrancer in good faith and for valuable consideration, shall—

(a) if the settlor is adjudicated bankrupt within two years after the date of the settlement, be void as against the Official Assignee, and

(b) if the settlor is adjudicated bankrupt at any subsequent time within five years after the date of the settlement, be void as against the Official Assignee unless the parties claiming under the settlement prove that the settlor was, at the time of making the settlement, able to pay all his debt without the aid of the property comprised in the settlement and that the interest of the settlor in such property passed to the trustee of such settlement on the execution thereof.

In *Re O'Neill* [1989] I.R. 544 at 551, Hamilton P. commented that "it is necessary that the conveyance should be both for valuable consideration and bona fide, or that the settlement should be one in consideration of marriage". In this case, the bankrupt conveyed his interest in his premises to his daughter at below market value, two years prior to him being declared bankrupt. The court held that the onus was on the Official Assignee to establish that the conveyance was made for the purpose of defrauding his creditors. Further, it was necessary that the assignee's daughter had been aware of the fraudulent purpose of the conveyance in order for it to be set aside.

The court in *Re Downes* [1898] 2 I.R. 635 held that the exception to settlements made in consideration of marriage can extend beyond the marriage of the settlor. In this case, a settlement in consideration of the settlor's sister was held to be covered by s.59 of the 1988 Act.

SETTLEMENTS DEFRAUDING CREDITORS

Generally, the purpose of such settlements is to prevent creditors from gaining access to property by transferring it to family members or others. Section 10 of the 1634 Act provides that any gift or conveyance of property, which is made for the purposes of delaying, hindering or defrauding creditors, is void as against such creditors. It should be noted that under s.14, this will not apply in instances where a conveyance is made bona fide for good consideration and without notice of any fraud.

In the case of *Bryce v Fleming* [1930] I.R. 376, the plaintiff obtained judgment against the defendant and registered it. The defendant then conveyed the land to a third party for the purpose of frustrating the judgment. Meredith J. noted that when it is clear that the conveyance is for good and valuable consideration and the purchaser is both acting bona fide and is unaware of the vendor's fraudulent intent, the conveyance will not be set aside under s.10. He stated at 383 that:

"... where there is a bona fide purchase for valuable consideration the transaction cannot be impeached under the operative section unless the purchaser is shown to have been privy to the vendor's intention."

The Court of Appeal in *Lloyds Bank Ltd v Marcan* [1973] 1 W.L.R. 339 was of the view that fraud involves some element of dishonesty, so while deceit is not a necessary element, dishonest intention is paramount. In this case, Pennycuick V.C. noted that in instances where valuable consideration falls short of full consideration, the onus rests on the purchaser to prove that he did not have the intention to defraud.

The judgment in *Re Moroney* [1887] 21 L.R. Ir. 27, suggests that there may be situations in which fraud may be proved within the meaning of s.10 of the 1634 Act without the presence of any actual dishonest intention on the part of the vendor. Costello P. adopted this reasoning in *McQuillan v Maguire* [1996] 1 I.L.R.M. 395, restating that the court did not have to find that the agreement had been motivated by fraudulent intent in order to deem it void.

Trustees

16

THE OFFICE OF TRUSTEE

This chapter will examine the nature of trustees' duties, powers and liabilities. The office of trustee is said to be burdensome in nature and in the performance of his office, a trustee must act wholly in the interest of the trust. The trustee stands to gain nothing from the trust, unless an express provision exists in the trust authorising remuneration. He is under an obligation to act with the highest standards of integrity and can be subjected to personal liability if that standard is not met. Generally, there is no minimum number of trustees required, except where statute requires otherwise (two trustees are required under s.39(1) of the Settled Land Act 1882 (repealed by the Land and Conveyancing Law Reform Act 2009 (the "2009 Act") Sch.2 Pt 4). For practical reasons it is preferable to appoint at least two. Furthermore, there is no upper limit on the number of trustees.

APPOINTMENT

The appointment of trustees may occur in a number of ways:

(i) A settlor may appoint a trustee when the trust is being created.
(ii) The power to appoint a trustee may be contained within the trust instrument.
(iii) Section 10 of the Trustee Act 1893 (the "1893 Act") is a statutory power providing for the appointment of trustees. It provides that this power can be exercised by "the person or persons nominated for the purpose of appointing new trustees by the instrument, if any, creating the trust, or if there is no such person or no such person able and willing to act, then the surviving or continuing trustees or trustee for the time being, or the personal representatives of the last surviving or continuing trustees".
This power is exercisable where the trustee:
(a) dies;
(b) remains outside the jurisdiction for a period exceeding 12 months;
(c) wishes to be discharged from his or her duties under the trust instrument;

(d) refuses to act in accordance with the trust instrument; or

(e) is deemed to be unfit or incapable of acting.

(iv) Section 25 of the 1893 Act empowers the court to appoint a trustee where it is expedient to do so and where it would be "inexpedient, difficult or impracticable so to do without the assistance of the court".

REMOVAL

Trustees can be removed in a number of ways:

(i) where there is express provision in the trust instrument;

(ii) where consent of all of the beneficiaries is obtained;

(iii) section 25 of the 1893 Act provides for the appointment of a new trustee in circumstances where an existing trustee is unfit or refuses to act; and

(iv) the High Court has an inherent jurisdiction to remove trustees where they act incompetently or dishonestly.

In the case of *Moore v McGlynn* [1894] 1 I.R. 74, the defendant was removed from his office as trustee in circumstances where he established a business that rivalled the business of the trust. It is not necessary that a trustee act dishonestly or with incompetence. A court has the jurisdiction to remove a trustee if it believes that it is in the best interests of the beneficiaries (see *Arnott v Arnott* [1924] 58 I.L.T.R. 145).

Barron J. in *Spencer v Kinsella* [1996] 2 I.L.R.M. 401 approved the decision in *Arnott v Arnott* and highlighted that the paramount consideration of the court when deciding whether or not to remove a trustee is the welfare of the beneficiaries of the trusts.

RETIREMENT

A person cannot be compelled to take up the office of trustee, however, if the appointment is accepted or not disclaimed within a reasonable period of time. The circumstances in which a trustee may retire are limited and are as follows:

(i) a trustee may retire on foot of an express provision in the trust instrument providing for it;

(ii) where there is agreement between all of the beneficiaries;

(iii) where replacement trustees are appointed under s.10 of the 1893 Act; and

(iv) section 11 of the 1893 Act provides for retirement in circumstances where at least two trustees remain and they consent to the retirement.

Duties of trustees

Upon appointment, trustees must ensure that they become acquainted with the terms of the trust and check the status of the trust property, i.e. whether the trust fund has been invested in accordance with the provisions of the trust instrument. Kekewich J. in *Hallows v Lloyd* [1888] 39 Ch D 686 stated that:

> "This raises the important question, what are the duties of persons becoming new trustees of a settlement? ... I think that when persons are asked to become new trustees, they are bound to enquire of what the property consists that is proposed to be handed over to them, and what are the trusts. They ought also to look into the trust documents and papers to ascertain what notices appear among them of encumbrances and other matters affecting the trust."

The duties of a trustee are extremely onerous and have to be carried out with the utmost diligence. If it is found that a trustee has failed to act in a responsible and reasonable manner, then they may be held personally liable for breach of trust. Central to a trustee's functions is the fiduciary duty that is imposed by equity. This duty places the trustee under a strict obligation to carry out the function of the trust with the utmost good faith. There are a number of specific duties that a trustee must consider in carrying out the office of trustee:

Investment

Unless the trust instrument contains an express investment clause, the duty to invest will be regulated by Pt I of the 1893 Act. Section 3 of the Act provides that the statutory power of investment is to be exercised at the trustee's discretion. The Trustee (Authorised Investments) Act 1958 specifies a list of authorised investments as well as giving the Minister the power to amend the list. The authorised list of investment was extended by the Trustee (Authorised Investments) Order 1998 (S.I. No. 28 of 1998) and now includes, inter alia, State securities, securities of semi-State bodies, and securities of financial institutions or other companies which are listed on a recognised stock exchange.

In *Re Harari's Settlement Trusts* [1949] 1 All E.R. 430, Jenkins J. was of the opinion that trustees can invest trust property "in or upon such investments as to them may seem fit". It seems, therefore, that trustees have the authority to invest in whatever manner they wish, provided they honestly believe that such investment is desirable.

It is important to note that even when a trustee stays within the authorised list of investments, either under the trust instrument itself or by statute, he must exercise the utmost prudence. In *Re O'Connor* [1913] 1 I.R. 69, O'Connor M.R. stated that:

> "[H]owever unlimited the power of investment may be, the trustee remains subject to the jurisdiction of the court. The trustee has not power to act dishonestly, negligently or in breach of trust to invest on insufficient security."

The standard of care and prudence that is expected of a trustee was considered by Lindley L.J. in *Learoyd v Whiteley* [1886] 33 Ch D 347, where he held that in addition to acting in a reasonable manner as would be expected from the prudent man investing on his own behalf, the trustee was obliged to take account of those for whom he was morally bound to provide.

A more flexible approach to the standard of care was adopted in the case of *Bartlett v Barclays Bank Trust Ltd* [1980] Ch. 515 at 531, where Brightman J. stated:

> "The cases establish that it is the duty of a trustee to conduct the business of the trust with the same care as an ordinary prudent man of business would extend towards his own affairs ... That does not mean that the trustee is bound to avoid all risk and in effect act as insurer of the trust fund."

Hoffmann J. in *Nestle v National Westminster Bank plc* [1993] 1 W.L.R. 1260 admitted that "trustees must act fairly in making investment decisions ...".

In *Stacey v Branch* [1995] 2 I.L.R.M. 136, Murphy J. held that the phrase "absolute discretion" that was contained in the trust instrument regarding the manner in which the trustee should invest the trust property did not relieve the trustee from his duty to use reasonable care and prudence.

It should be noted that trustees may pursue an ethical investment policy provided that such investments are not financially disadvantageous to the beneficiaries. The question of ethical investment is most relevant to trusts that are charitable in nature. In *Harries v Church Commissioners* [1993] 2 All E.R. 300, Nicholls V.C. understood that the law will not require a trustee to make an investment that would bring the charity into disrepute; however, an element of prudence must be maintained so as not to make moral statements at the expense of the beneficiaries.

DUTY NOT TO MAKE A PROFIT

It is a well-established principle that a trustee may not profit from his position unless provision is expressly made for same in the trust instrument. This principle is to prevent the trustee from making any secret profit from the trust or any financial benefit that is not authorised by the trust instrument. Section 24 of the Trustee Act 1893 provides that a trustee "may reimburse himself, or pay or discharge out of the trust premises all expenses incurred in or about the execution of his trusts or powers".

O'Sullivan v Management Agency and Music Ltd [1985] Q.B. 428 is authority for the proposition that the courts have an inherent jurisdiction to authorise the payment of remuneration for work done.

Subject to narrow exceptions, a trustee is prohibited from purchasing any property belonging to the trust, as he would effectively be vendor and purchaser. "Self-dealing" as it is commonly known is voidable at the instance of any beneficiary, however fair and reasonable the transaction. Megarry V.C. in *Tito v Wadell (No. 2)* [1977] Ch. 106 at 241 stated that:

> "The self-dealing rule is … that if a trustee sells the trust property to himself, the sale is voidable by any beneficiary *ex debito justitae*, however fair the transaction."

In cases where the trustee purchases property from the beneficiary directly, rather than the trust, the "fair dealing rule" applies. This states that there exists a presumption of undue influence that may be rebutted by the trustee demonstrating that no advantage has been taken and that the transaction is fair and honest (see *Smyth v Smyth*, unreported, High Court, Costello J., November 22, 1978).

DUTY TO KEEP ACCOUNTS AND PROVIDE INFORMATION

Trustees are under an obligation to keep accurate accounts of the trust property, with the beneficiaries having a right to inspect such accounts. Kenny J. in *Chaine-Nickson v Bank of Ireland* [1976] I.R. 393 at 396 held that:

> "When a beneficiary has a vested interest in a trust fund so that he has a right of payment of the income, the trustees must at all reasonable times at this request give him full and accurate information as to the amount and state of the trust property and permit him or his solicitor, to inspect the accounts and vouchers and other documents relating to the trust."

In *Murphy v Murphy* [1999] 1 W.L.R. 282, Neuberger J. followed Kenny J. in *Chaine-Nickson*, but refused to grant access to trust accounts in circumstances where they were being sought by a potential beneficiary. Here, as the plaintiff was merely a potential beneficiary along with the rest of the world, he was not entitled to relief.

The Court of Appeal in *Re Londonderry's Settlement* [1965] Ch. 918 held that beneficiaries under a discretionary trust are not entitled to demand that trustees furnish them with the reasons as to why the trust property was distributed in a certain manner. The most recent decision in *Breakspear v Ackland* [2009] Ch. 32 suggests that while the principle of confidentiality laid down in *Londonderry* is still good law, the increasing significance of accountability may lead to a greater degree of disclosure than might previously have been contemplated.

DUTY TO DISTRIBUTE

Trustees are under an obligation to properly distribute the trust property as per the trust instrument. The identity of all beneficiaries must be ascertained prior to distribution as any beneficiary who receives no money or is underpaid as a result of the failure of the trustee to identify them has a right of action against that trustee. An application to court for directions can be made where trustees are in any doubt in relation to the claims of beneficiaries and they will be protected from liability if they follow the court's directions.

In circumstances where it is unknown whether a beneficiary is alive, or his whereabouts are unknown, the court can authorise distribution after a certain period of time. This procedure is commonly known as a "Benjamin order" and can be granted when a period of seven years has elapsed after the last contact with the beneficiary. In *Re Benjamin* [1902] 1 Ch. 723, the testator's son had disappeared some 10 years earlier, a year prior to his father's death. In circumstances where the missing son was a beneficiary of his father's will, Joyce J. held that the son must be presumed dead and permitted the trustees to distribute the estate.

DUTY TO CONVERT TRUST PROPERTY

This duty imposes an obligation on trustees to maintain equality between different types of beneficiaries. Conversion relates to the way in which trust property is held and how it has to be adjusted. The duty arises in two instances. First, if there is an express trust for sale, the trustee has an obligation to sell the property in a timely manner. Secondly, the rule in *Howe v Earl of Darthmouth* [1802] 7 Ves. Jr. 137 applies where there exists a duty to convert; the purpose of such rule being to maintain equality between current beneficiaries and future beneficiaries. The rule was summarised by Walker J. in *Re Harris* [1907] 1 I.R. 32 at 35:

> "The general rule is, that where there is a general residuary bequest of personal estate, including chattels real, to be enjoyed by persons in succession, the Court put upon the bequest the interpretation that the

persons indicated are to enjoy the same thing in succession, and converts the property as the only means of giving effect to that intention."

Non-delegation

The principle of non-delegation prevents trustees from transferring their duties under the trust to third parties. The office of trustees is one which cannot be delegated to another as it is personal to the person who was appointed under the trust. That said, the trust instrument may specifically provide for delegation. It was stated by Lord Langdale M.R. in *Turner v Corney* [1841] 5 Beav. 515 at 517 that "trustees who take on themselves the management of property for the benefit of others have no right to shift their duty on other persons".

It is of course possible for a trustee to delegate certain functions to professional advisors, such as solicitors and accountants. However, such delegation is on the proviso that the trustee exercises a reasonable degree of supervision over the third party.

Powers of trustees

Trustees may exercise such powers as are bestowed upon them by the trust instrument or by the 1893 Act. A power can be distinguished from a duty, in that it is discretionary and not compulsory.

Power of sale

Trustees have no inherent power to sell trust property. The power must come from:
  (i) the trust instrument;
  (ii) statute; or
  (iii) court order.

The rule in *Howe v Earl of Darthmouth* stipulates that if a trust is created which settles property other than realty on persons in succession and where the assets constitute unauthorised securities or are wasting in nature, the trustees are obliged to sell the property.

Section 13 of the 1893 Act gives wide discretion to trustees as to the manner in which the sale is to be carried out, for example by auction, private sale or tender.

Section 14 empowers trustees to sell property that is subject to depreciation. Unlike the rule in *Howe v Earl of Darthmouth*, this section also applies to real property.

Section 20 empowers trustees to provide receipts for the sale of trust property. The receipt has the effect of absolving the purchaser from any liability in the circumstance where the trustee is acting in breach of the trust instrument.

It is important to note that s.20(1) of the Land and Conveyancing Law Reform Act 2009 now provides that: "[s]ubject to—(a) the duties of a trustee, and (b) any restrictions imposed by any statutory provision (including this Act) or the general law of trusts or by any instrument or court order relating to the land, a trustee of land has the full power of an owner to convey or otherwise deal with it."

POWERS OF MAINTENANCE AND ADVANCEMENT

Trusts commonly make provision for the maintenance of infants through the income generated by trust property. The trustee's power to do this may arise from the trust instrument or statute. Advancement, on the other hand, relates to the possibility of the trustees permitting part of the trust capital to be paid or used for the benefit of a beneficiary prior to his interest becoming vested.

Section 43 of the Conveyancing Act 1881 empowers trustees to apply trust income for the maintenance of infant beneficiaries. The section permits the maintenance to be paid to the infant's parent or guardian.

Section 11 of the Guardianship of Infants Act 1964 makes provision for the advancement of trust property. The court has an inherent jurisdiction to authorise the payment of income or capital for the education or maintenance of the infant. Maguire P. in *Re O'Neill* [1943] I.R. 564 at 565 stated that:

> "I must be satisfied that such a course is not only beneficial but necessary to the welfare of the minors ... The jurisdiction to make an advancement out of capital is not to be exercised lightly. Where a minor is actually destitute the way is clear, but where the minors ... are not destitute, the question of the existence of a sufficient element of necessity becomes a difficult problem."

LIABILITY OF TRUSTEES FOR BREACH OF TRUST

A trustee is both liable for his acts of omission and acts of commission. In circumstances where a trustee fails to exercise the required degree of supervision of the trust, he may be liable to make good the losses that the trust has suffered, once the beneficiaries can establish breach of trust. Further, a trustee may be called to account for any profit that he has made as a result of the breach.

Generally, trustees are only liable for their own breaches and not those of co-trustees. However, a failure to intervene to prevent known breaches of the trust by co-trustees may attract liability.

In *Head v Gould* [1898] 2 Ch. 250, it was held that where an unauthorised investment is improperly retained by a trustee, the measure of compensation will amount to the difference between the price that the asset would have realised if sold at the appropriate time and the actual selling price of the asset.

Where an authorised investment is improperly disposed of, the measure of the trustee's liability will be the costs of repurchase of the investment at the current market rate.

In *Target Holdings v Redferns* [1996] A.C. 421, Lord Browne-Wilkinson stated that:

> "The quantum is fixed at the date of judgment at which date, according to the circumstances then pertaining, the compensation is assessed at the figure that is necessary to put the trust estate or the beneficiary back in the position it would have been in had there been no breach."

It should be noted that where a trustee has committed a breach of trust, it is a defence if the said breach was instigated by, participated in or consented to by the beneficiaries (see *Re Pauling's Settlement Trusts* [1962] 1 W.L.R. 86).

VARIATION OF TRUSTS

Part 5 (ss.23 and 24) of the 2009 Act makes specific statutory provision for the first time in Irish law for the variation of trusts. It is important to note that Pt 5 is not limited in its application to trusts involving land. Prior to the 2009 Act, with very limited exceptions, the law prohibited variations in trusts.

Section 24 establishes the new jurisdiction, which permits an "appropriate person" to make an application to court for an order to approve an arrangement for the benefit of a "relevant person".

A "relevant person" is defined as the person for whose benefit a variation may be sought, with the definition of "relevant trust" excluding both charitable and pension trusts from the jurisdiction under Pt 5.

Four categories of "relevant person" are recognised:

- a person who is incapable by reason of infancy or absence of mental capacity;
- an unborn person;
- a person whose identity, existence or whereabouts cannot reasonably be established;

- a person with a contingent interest under a trust who is not an infant or under a disability (for example a recalcitrant adult beneficiary).

For the court to exercise its jurisdiction, the proposed arrangement must have been assented to in writing by any other beneficiaries, excluding any "relevant persons", who are capable of assenting. The court may not approve an application in any case where these conditions are not fulfilled or where the Revenue Commissioners have satisfied the court that the application is substantially motivated by a desire to avoid or reduce tax liability.

Tracing

17

TRACING AT COMMON LAW

Traditionally, tracing at common law allowed property to be traced into the possession of another, provided that the property remained identifiable. The common law is unable to trace into mixed funds and is consequently very restrictive. Therefore, once money is mixed, as in a bank account, there can be no tracing at common law.

The common law approach to tracing was well summarised by Millett J. in *Agip (Africa) v Jackson* [1990] Ch. 265 at 285:

> "The common law has always been able to follow a physical asset from one recipient to another ... It can follow money but not a chose in action. Money can be followed at common law into and out of a bank account and into the hands of a subsequent transferee, provided that it does not cease to be identifiable by being mixed with other money in the bank account derived from some other source ..."

Only identifiable assets can be followed and as was seen in the case of *Taylor v Plummer* [1815] 3 M. & S. 562 at 575, only stock that was incorrectly purchased with the plaintiff's money was held to belong to the plaintiff, with Lord Ellenborough stating that:

> "[I]t makes no difference in reason or law into what other form, different from the original, the change may have been made ... [T]he product of or substitute for the original thing still follows the nature of the thing itself, as long as it can be ascertained as such."

TRACING IN EQUITY

A new understanding of tracing is that it is neither a right nor a remedy. Tracing in equity is believed to be a more powerful and flexible tool. Equitable tracing is an obvious exception to the rule that equity acts in personam as equitable tracing is a proprietary remedy.

TRACING

It should be noted that tracing is distinct from the procedure known as following, which involves the following of a distinct asset into the possession of another. On the other hand, tracing is required when the distinct asset is transferred into the possession of another and that person exchanges it for another asset. The distinction between tracing and following was examined by Lord Millet in *Foskett v McKeown* [2000] 2 W.L.R. 1299 at 1322:

> "The process of ascertaining what happened to the plaintiff's money involves both tracing and following. These are both exercises in locating assets which are or may be taken to represent an asset belonging to the plaintiffs and to which they assert ownership. The process of following and tracing are, however, distinct. Following is the process of following the same asset as it moves from hand to hand. Tracing is the process of identifying a new asset into the hands of the new owner or to trace its value into the new asset in the hands of the same owner."

The procedure of tracing permits one asset to stand in place of another. It is possible to follow monies into a mixed fund and then to trace an asset that was purchased with the mixed fund.

TRACING INTO BANK ACCOUNTS

In circumstances where trust monies are mixed into a bank account, equity provides for the tracing of those monies.

Clayton's Case [1816] 1 Mer. 572 is authority for the proposition that a bank account is treated as a series of debts, with the debt that is first in time being discharged before the other debts. This is commonly known as the "first in, first out" rule or the rule in *Clayton's Case*.

In *Re Hallett's Estate* [1880] 13 Ch D 696, the court concluded that the rule in *Clayton's Case* is subject to any contrary intention of the parties.

In the case of *Barlow Clowes International v Vaughan* [1992] 4 All E.R. 22, the Court of Appeal departed from the rule in circumstances where it was inconsistent with the intentions of investors.

Laffoy J. in *Re Money Markets International Stockbrokers Ltd* [1999] 4 I.R. 267 held that the rule in *Clayton's case* was prima facie applicable although it may be departed from in circumstances where it is not in concurrence with the intentions of the beneficiaries of a trust fund. See also, *Headstart Global Fund Ltd v Citco Bank Nederland NV* [2011] IEHC 5.

Furthermore, it is possible to trace into a bank account by way of an overdrawn account or debt. However, it is essential that the asset purchased with the account funds be identifiable.

In general terms, tracing in equity would only extend to persons that are in fiduciary relationships. The position was commented on by Millett J. in *Agip (Africa) v Jackson* [1990] Ch. 265 at 290 as follows:

> "The only restriction on the ability of equity to follow assets is the requirement that there must be some fiduciary relationship which permits the assistance of equity to be invoked ... The requirement may be circumvented since it is not necessary that the fund to be traced should have been the subject of fiduciary obligations before it got into the wrong hands; it is sufficient that the payment to the defendant itself gives rise to a fiduciary relationship: *Chase Manhattan Bank NA v Israel-British Bank London Ltd* [1981] Ch. 105."

More recently, in the case of *Boscawn v Bajwa* [1996] 1 W.L.R. 328 at 335, Millett L.J. was of the opinion that "it is still a prerequisite of the right to trace that there must be a fiduciary relationship which calls the equitable jurisdiction into being".

Loss of the right to trace

The loss of the right to trace may occur in a number of circumstances.

First, in circumstances where the property has been dissipated it will not be possible to trace. Lord Greene in *Re Diplock* [1948] Ch. 465 at 521 stated:

> "The equitable remedies presuppose the continued existence of the money either as a separate fund or as part of a mixed fund or as latent in property acquired by means of such a fund. If, on the facts of any individual case, such continued existence is not established, equity is as helpless as the common law itself. If the fund mixed or unmixed, is spent upon a dinner, equity, which dealt only in specific relief and not in damages, could do nothing."

Secondly, tracing will be unavailable if a bona fide purchaser for value without notice acquires the property. Thirdly, no claimant can trace who has acquiesced in the wrongful mixing or distribution of property. Lastly, tracing will not be allowed where it causes inequity.

TRACING

FOLLOWING

Following is quite straightforward in circumstances where an identifiable asset is merely transferred from one party to another. Complications arise where the asset becomes mixed with other assets. It is possible for a claimant to follow his assets into the mixture and assert that his contribution exits as part of the mixture. In circumstances where there is a reduction in the mixture, any claim will be reduced in proportion to the relative contributions.

In *Re Hallett's Estate* [1880] 13 Ch. 696 at 727, a solicitor misapplied funds held by him in trust, by paying them into his own bank account. Sir George Jessel M.R. ruled that:

> "When we come to apply that principle to the case of a trustee who has blended trust moneys with his own, it seems to me perfectly plain that he cannot be heard to say that he took away the trust money when he had a right to take away his own money."

Budd J. in *Shanahan's Stamp Auctions v Farrelly* [1962] I.R. 386 at 428 was of the opinion that "it would appear therefore that Hallet's Case establishes certain principles ... If money held by a person in a fiduciary capacity, though not a trustee, has been paid into his bank account, it can be followed by the beneficiary".

CLAIMING

Claiming is a procedure that is distinct from tracing and following. It is entirely dependent upon the extent of the rights that a claimant is asserting against an asset. When the beneficial owner of an asset has followed it into the possession of another, he may assert his equitable ownership and obtain an order compelling the defendant to restore the asset to him.

In circumstances where the asset is transferred into a mixed fund, the claimant may either assert a charge over the fund or assert an entitlement to a share of the fund which is proportionate to his contribution. In the House of Lords case of *Foskett v McKeown* [2000] 2 W.L.R. 1299 at 1325, Lord Millett stated that:

> "The simplest case is where a trustee wrongfully misappropriates trust property and uses it exclusively to acquire other property for his own benefit. In such a case the beneficiary is entitled at his option either to assert his beneficial ownership of the proceeds or to bring a personal claim against the trustee for breach of trust and enforce an equitable lien or charge on the proceeds to secure restoration of the trust fund."

Index

INDEX

PHILIPS
AVENT

42133 5440 271